CW01511075

Capricorn
23 December – 20 January

DID YOU PURCHASE THIS BOOK WITHOUT A COVER?

If you did, you should be aware it is **stolen property** as it was reported *unsold and destroyed* by a retailer. Neither the author nor the publisher has received any payment for this book.

All Rights Reserved including the right of reproduction in whole or in part in any form. This edition is published by arrangement with Harlequin Enterprises II B.V./S.à.r.l. The text of this publication or any part thereof may not be reproduced or transmitted in any form or by any means, electronic or mechanical, including photocopying, recording, storage in an information retrieval system, or otherwise, without the written permission of the publisher.

This book is sold subject to the condition that it shall not, by way of trade or otherwise, be lent, resold, hired out or otherwise circulated without the prior consent of the publisher in any form of binding or cover other than that in which it is published, and without a similar condition including this condition being imposed on the subsequent purchaser.

® and ™ are trademarks owned and used by the trademark owner and/or its licensee. Trademarks marked with ® are registered with the United Kingdom Patent Office and/or the Office for Harmonisation in the Internal Market and in other countries.

First published in Great Britain 2010
by Harlequin Mills & Boon Limited,
Eton House, 18-24 Paradise Road, Richmond, Surrey TW9 1SR

Copyright © Dadhichi Toth 2007, 2008, 2009, 2010 & 2011

ISBN: 978 0 263 87387 0

Typeset at Midland Typesetters Australia

Harlequin Mills & Boon policy is to use papers that are natural, renewable and recyclable products and made from wood grown in sustainable forests. The logging and manufacturing processes conform to the legal environmental regulations of the country of origin.

Printed and bound in Spain
by Litografia Rosés S.A., Barcelona

About
Dadhichi

Dadhichi is one of Australia's foremost astrologers. He has the ability to draw from complex astrological theory to provide clear, easily understandable advice and insights for people who want to know what their futures might hold.

In the 27 years that Dadhichi has been practising astrology, face reading and other esoteric studies, he has conducted over 9,500 consultations. His clients include celebrities, political and diplomatic figures, and media and corporate identities from all over the world.

Dadhichi's unique blend of astrology and face reading helps people fulfil their true potential. His extensive experience in western astrology is complemented by his research into the theory and practice of eastern systems of astrology.

Dadhichi is a regular columnist for several Australian magazines. He often appears as a guest on leading Australian television and radio networks, where many of his political and world-wide forecasts have proved uncannily accurate.

His websites www.astrology.com.au, www.facereader.com, www.soulconnector.com and www.psychjuice.com attract hundreds of thousands of visitors each month, and offer a wide variety of features, helpful information and services.

Dedicated to The Light of Intuition

Sri V. Krishnaswamy—mentor and friend

With thanks to Julie, Joram, Isaac and Janelle

Welcome from
Dadhichi

Dear Friend,

Welcome to your astrological forecast for 2011! I've spent considerable time preparing these insights for you. My goal is to give you an overview of your sign and I hope you can use my simple suggestions to steer you in the right direction.

I am often asked by my clients to help them understand their true path and what they are supposed to be doing in life. This is a complex task; however, astrology can assist with finding some answers. In this book I attempt to reveal those unique character traits that define who you are. With a greater self-understanding, you can effectively begin *to live who you are* rather than wondering about *what you should do*. Identity is the key!

Knowing when the best opportunities in your life are likely to appear is the other benefit of astrology, based on planetary transits and forecasting. The latter part of the book deals with what is *likely* to happen on a yearly, monthly and daily basis. By coupling this section with the last chapter, an effective planner, you can conduct your business, relationships and personal affairs in ways that yield maximum benefits for you.

Along with your self-knowledge, there are two other key attitudes you must carry with you: *trust* and *courage*. Unless you're prepared to take a gamble in life, earnestly and fearlessly, you'll stay stuck in the same place, never really growing or progressing. At some point you have to take a step forward. When you synchronise yourself with the powerful talents found in your Sun sign, you'll begin to understand what your mission in life will be. This is the true purpose and use of astrology.

So I invite you to gear up for an exciting fifteen months! Don't shrink back from life, even if at times some of the forecasts seem a little daunting. Don't forget that humans are always at their best when the going gets tough. The difficult planetary transits are merely invitations to bring out the best in yourself, while the favourable planetary cycles are seasons for enjoying the benefits that karma has in store for you.

Remain positive, expect the best, and see the beauty in everyone and everything. Remember the words of a great teacher: 'The world is as you see it.' In other words, life will reflect back to you only what you are willing to see.

I trust the coming fifteen months will grant you wonderful success, health, love and happiness. May the light of the Sun, the Moon and all of the stars fill your heart with joy and satisfaction.

Your Astrologer,

Dadhichi Toth

Contents

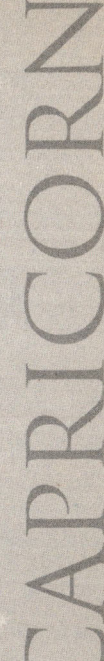
CAPRICORN

The Capricorn
Identity

*And in the end, it's not the years in your life that
count. It's the life in your years.*

—Abraham Lincoln

Capricorn: A Snapshot

Key Characteristics

Conventional, reserved, practical, dedicated, ambitious,
controlling, suspicious

Compatible Star Signs

Taurus, Virgo, Cancer, Scorpio and Pisces

Key Life Phrase

I acquire

Life Goals

To achieve financial security and material independence

Platinum Assets

Ambition, drive and steadiness

Zodiac Totem

The Goat

Zodiac Symbol

♑

Zodiac Facts

Tenth sign of the zodiac; cardinal, barren, feminine, dry

Element

Earth

Famous Capricorns

Christy Turlington, Denzel Washington,
Carolyn Bessette Kennedy, J.R.R. Tolkien, David Bowie,
Elvis Presley, Naomi Judd, Kirstie Alley, Faye Dunaway,
Martin Luther King Jr, Howard Hughes, Muhammad Ali,
Kevin Costner, Edgar Allan Poe, Tiger Woods,
Jon Voight, Mel Gibson

Capricorn: Your profile

Capricorn is the cardinal earth sign of the zodiac and can be likened to the oldest and most valuable tree in the forest. You are sure-footed and thoroughly practical. In the end, the Capricorn goat always reaches the top of the mountain by beating others who may initially be faster but are less determined.

Yours is the tenth sign, an earthy element, which makes you realistic and matter of fact. Saturn, your ruling planet, gives you an edge of caution and you are sometimes shy and lack self-confidence or self-esteem.

You have great practical skills; material, financial and social resources that can be used to further your ambitions. You are not afraid of hard work to achieve what you want in life and, when you find what it is you are aiming for, you will keep going until you succeed.

Although you like money, you prefer to know exactly where your hard-earned dollars are going, so risky ventures are not for you. You have excellent organisational skills and will work away quietly and surely without attracting too much attention to yourself.

For you to be interested in a project, it has to have a solid grounding because airy-fairy concepts are beyond your understanding. When you are given a job to do, you tend to ignore the clock and simply work away quietly, without fuss and not wasting any time. Commitment comes naturally to you and you are likely to be successful at whatever you attempt.

Although people may not generally see you as enthusiastic when they first meet you, after a while they will see the side of you that is humorous and affectionate. Initially you may come across as rather cool, but will thaw out when you get to know others a little better. You like to understand where the other person is coming from with their ideas and they will be regarded with suspicion until they pass your rather stringent character tests.

It is often the case that Capricorns are not properly supported early in their lives and so learn from a young age how to be self-sufficient and go it alone. You feel that self-sufficiency adds to your strength and do not ask others to carry you, either personally or professionally. Added to this, of course, is that you like to take full credit for whatever work you do and the goals you have achieved.

Capricorns are level-headed, but they are not all that optimistic about life in general. They tend to be more of the 'cup half-empty' type of person than the 'cup half-full'. The phrase expect the worst, but hope for the best may be constantly playing somewhere in the back of your mind.

A typical Capricorn is fearful of being embarrassed in public and, although they may tap their toes in time to the music, getting up and being the centre of attention on the dance floor or deliberately making a fool of themselves is too much for them to consider.

A lifestyle based on tradition appeals to you because you like things in their place and need to be in control. It would rarely be said that you are the most exciting person to be around, but you are very loyal and will never let anyone down once you have given your word. Adventure is best left to others as far as you are concerned. You would rather live life on your own terms than compromise and live as others would like you to.

You are generous with your time and money. If a worthy cause is presented to you, your generosity knows no bounds. There are few other star signs who are as good a judge of character as you are, Capricorn. You are not blind to the manipulation and secrecy others use to get their own way. With your naturally in-built, suspicious nature, you can usually work out what dubious characters are up to and not get embroiled in their latest get-rich-quick scheme.

If you give your word in a partnership, whether personal or professional, it is absolutely binding. You are trustworthy, dependent and punctual and can always be counted on to fulfil the contract you have shaken hands on. You expect people to be just as trustworthy as you are; but, unfortunately, this is not always the case.

You are likely to have success later in life, and when it does come to you, you will share what you have achieved with others. Success to you is measured in what worldly goods you have accumulated.

You are resilient. Because your childhood has usually been difficult, you are able to weather the storms of life and come out the other side into calm waters with considerable strength intact. It is not in your nature to give up easily and you become emotionally stronger as life throws more and more challenges your way.

Your totem is the goat, the agile animal who can balance impossibly on rocky and almost vertical surfaces. At times, your life seems to mirror this exact territory. But also, like the goat, it is highly unlikely that you will fall from your mountain because you are sure-footed in everything you do. Although you are courageous in your own way, there will be no dashing off on some unlikely adventure for you, Capricorn, and that is just the way you like your world to be.

Three classes of Capricorn

Those of you born between the 23rd of December and the 1st of January are a strong-minded group of Capricorns, who are exceedingly ambitious in the way they express themselves. You are most likely to find success and happiness through your work. Marriage and family life is also important to you, but may take second place to your work.

If you were born between the 2nd and the 11th of January you are inflexible, which will be particularly challenging for your relationships. You are also somewhat possessive and jealous. However, you are extremely practical and your commonsense will be one of your most invaluable assets.

If you were born between the 12th and 20th of January, your mind is brilliant and full of amazing details and plans. You see the minutiae of each and every situation. You are a little critical of yourself and others and perhaps should spend a little more time focusing on your good points rather than your bad.

Capricorn role model: David Bowie

David Bowie isn't a typical Capricorn because of his obvious artistic and musical talents. Capricorn is, however, stongly linked to Venus and due to this connection he has a wonderful creative flair. He also has a knack for success and re-inventing himself which has made him timelessly popular.

Capricorn: The light side

Those born under the zodiac sign of Capricorn are indeed self-sufficient and blessed with sharp intellect. Your practical mind will generally get it right the first time around, even though it may take a little longer to process an idea, due to your fear of making a fool of yourself.

You make a great leader and know that actions often speak louder than words. People also know you give considerable thought to an idea before it even sees the light of day. Withholding your decisions until you are ready to release them may expose you to criticism; however, you handle pressure superbly and this again reinforces the idea that everything a Capricorn does is definitely under control.

In fashion you prefer traditional styles because you have your eye on quality and the long-term benefits this will bring. You are down-to-earth and therefore are averse to showing off, so at first people may not recognise that you are graceful, beautiful and elegantly dressed.

Power fascinates you, but you will use your own justly. Most Capricorns mete out judgement and punishment in a reasonable manner because they like to play fair. However, if people cross you or deceive you, then you may not let things go all that easily.

Capricorn: The shadow side

Although you have a real knack for judging people, this can also be coupled with your tendency to be rather picky about another person's character. You may even store this information away until a time when you can use it against them, either personally or professionally. Be careful that this doesn't become an automatic response when meeting new people for the first time, because you should also try to be as constructive as possible in your criticism of others. We are human, not perfect.

Your reputation is extremely important to you, but it should not be the number one priority in your life. Achieving wealth and influence is a basic need in your character, but it shouldn't be the driving force to the detriment of everything else. Balance is what is needed.

Taking risks doesn't come naturally to you and can, in fact, make you feel quite uncomfortable. By closing your mind to something that is a little out of left field you may miss out on wonderful opportunities in your home life or business. Don't let the love of money and what it can buy blind you to other options and what they can offer.

Capricorn woman

You are very ladylike, Capricorn, and dress in a way that is stylish, elegant and graceful. You also dress according to what you are planning to achieve that day, whether personal or professional. You may at first be overlooked as not being quite as glamorous as your peers, but this is not at all true. As a Capricorn female, you will grow and mature into a truly beautiful woman. You have a subtle beauty and grace that most other star signs lack.

Capricorn is a deep and mystical sign and, even though most people assume that your primary driving force in life is to amass wealth, they would be unwise to ignore your other qualities. You may seem a little aloof when people first encounter you, but you tend to hold back and wait for the other person to prove their worth, honesty and integrity before holding out your welcoming hand.

Perceptive people will find that behind your rather stand-offish façade, you have a good, kind heart and a personality that is rich and deep for those who are lucky enough to have you as a friend. You are loyal to those you care about, utterly trustworthy and as steady as the rock on which your totem the goat climbs.

Taking on a complicated task doesn't faze you at all and some men may be in awe of your ability to achieve the ambitions you have outlined for yourself. You are confident you can handle any job at hand, having no problem competing with members of the opposite sex. Although they may not feel the same way about you! This fierce competitiveness may even spill over into your personal life and could become an obstacle to your romantic happiness.

To your way of thinking we are all created equal and you feel that hard work and survival of the fittest are the ways of the world in the 21st century. You are more than capable of managing on your own when working because most likely you have thought a project through before beginning it and know exactly what you need to do. Your experiences of self-sufficiency during early childhood will stand you in good stead in this kind of situation.

Your friendly planet Venus indicates you have an entertaining and comical side to your personality that others rarely see. You have a tendency to take life a bit too seriously, so take some leisure time to see such forms of artistic expression as the theatre or movies that will entertain and brighten your day.

They say that laughter is the best medicine, so give it a try.

You may not be a domestic goddess, finding all that cleaning and dusting rather tedious, but you do like to live in a tidy, well-ordered home. Paying someone else to do the chores that you really dislike may be a way of distributing some of your hard-earned dollars.

It is difficult, even almost impossible, to bulldoze a Capricorn into making a quick or frivolous decision. But once you've made up your mind and have a clear idea of what you want and exactly how to get it, you'll stick to it, 100 per cent. Your word is your honour. You have great strength and the mental ability to carry out any task you have resolved to do.

You don't find it difficult to delegate to others, but only after you have completely checked them out and they have passed your rather tough tests. It is important to have a team around you who are all paddling in the same direction so that your goals can be achieved.

Capricorn man

It would be difficult indeed to ignore the air of authority exuded by the Capricorn male. Saturn is the conservative but hard taskmaster responsible for this trait. Being in control is where you prefer to be and this is part and parcel of your Capricorn personality. You have a strong air of confidence and are generally respected by those around you because you believe that respect is to be earned.

From a very young age you are confident that you will be a success and start to dream about what you can achieve in the way of material satisfaction and security well before any of your peers even know what it means. You are a natural businessman and a love of financial security is part of your nature from the time you are born.

When you were young, you may have been seen as dour for your age, because the purpose of doing anything silly is beyond your comprehension. But as you gain in years and your security grows, you'll become more comfortable in your own skin, start to relax and enjoy life much more. In a way, you get younger as you get older.

You love working, having a sense of achievement, of attaining your goals, and are in danger of becoming a workaholic. It is very rewarding to do a job well, but it is just as important to have a balanced life; otherwise, why work so hard? It is all right to earn big dollars, but what is the point if there is no one there to share your success?

You may have many acquaintances in your life but will probably have only a few very close friends who understand how sensitive and caring you are beneath a seemingly cold, hard exterior. You will be loyal, generous and put yourself out to do anything for your friends. However, just as you give loyalty out, so too you will expect the same in return.

Along life's path you will learn that sometimes things are not as easily achieved as you initially thought they would be and, if you have had a hard or difficult upbringing, issues of trust may impinge upon you. If you can appreciate what you have and be a little easier on yourself, you may actually be able to smell the roses without being too hung up on the thorns.

You are an old soul, Capricorn, born with an uncanny wisdom about the world. You listen very carefully to your gut feelings and have a well developed intuition that does, on countless occasions, serve you well. Because you rarely make an instant decision about anyone or anything, this gives you time to listen intently to your inner voice, which is a very useful thing to have, especially in business.

You are regarded by others as a rather solitary individual, but are not necessarily lonely. You are quite happy to work away on your own and gain great pleasure from your efforts. Young male Capricorns may seem much older than their years when expressing their opinions on financial, political and social matters. You tend to be more conservative than your peers and this is largely because you want a secure future, free of worry and monetary concerns.

Capricorn child

If you are the parent of a Capricorn child, you may come to notice that more than one person will make the observation that your child has an old head on young shoulders. Capricorn youngsters are mature beyond their years and may seem as if they have been 'here' before, so wise are they at such a young age.

The Capricorn child will give you a power struggle that not many other children are capable of. They usually get what they want, when they want it. They are quite clear about what they want, too, so it is a waste of time beating around the bush. Often it is much simpler to ask what they would like first off and they'll be more than happy to tell you.

A Capricorn child may even prefer older company because they have a wise head on their shoulders. They have a mind that is inquisitive and usually working well ahead of the set agenda for the day. To understand your Capricorn child, you need to be able to read their body language because they are not always verbal when they are unhappy or dissatisfied. Their eyes will also tell you a lot about how they are feeling.

They are emotional beings and need to be taught how to unwind and enjoy themselves. They need to be taught that achieving their goals is only half the equation and the other half is being able to laugh and have fun in the process. They do well with lots of fresh air and physical activity, to help reduce their stress levels.

Capricorn children are generally good at school, focused on the tasks at hand and enjoy having a good reputation. Their work will be completed to the best of their ability and handed in on time. At times they may feel they're not working hard enough, so you must help them to relax while simultaneously keeping up your encouragement to do their best work. This is a fine line to tread, but when done with love and patience, they will blossom and grow into confident, well-rounded adults.

They need a secure and comfortable home to remain happy and harmonious. Because they are worriers they can get depressed if they keep problems to themselves. Talking about their private issues is not easy for them, but they should be encouraged to do so in a safe and familiar environment. Because they aim so high, it is easy for them to feel they've failed, even when they have done exceptionally well.

Romance, love and marriage

Capricorn, you can be so involved in achieving your grand plan that, when a romantic opportunity comes along and stares you right in the face, you may not even recognise what's happening until it is too late and that potential life partner has disappeared over the horizon, hand in hand with someone else!

You have very clear ideas of your romantic ideals, just as you do with everything else. However, your criteria may be a little hard for the average person to match, so any prospective partner must be unafraid to pass some of your rather severe tests to prove their love to you. Just don't make the bar so high that anyone not equipped with wings can't jump over it!

You may be a bit slow off the mark when making an approach to a potential partner; a bit shy and awkward, because you are a private person. But at the end of the day, everyone needs to have someone special in their life, don't they? These shy traits can make you miss out on wonderful opportunities again and again, especially when younger.

Many females born under Capricorn are seen as not keeping up with modern attitudes, preferring a more conventional approach where the male takes the lead. You don't really subscribe to the oft-repeated phrase, 'when our eyes met across the room, it was love at first sight'. This is a little too fanciful for you, Capricorn. You prefer to take your time, savouring each meeting, until you've made up your mind. You are extremely faithful when you do tie the knot—however long it may take.

More than any other sign, you need to be aware of an opportunity when it comes along. It is difficult for you to say 'I love you' to just anyone and you must feel financially secure to put your heart on your sleeve. Your life partner will have to have integrity, be hard working, and as committed as you are to the relationship. For all these reasons it may take a few years for you to find that person who you believe is your true soulmate.

You may get to a point in your life where you feel you have tried so many times to find the love that works for you, but don't give up! Yes, you're traditional, perhaps a little old-fashioned, but when it comes to giving yourself to the right one, you'll do so completely in body, mind and soul. For a partner, this is worth waiting for.

On the other hand, if you have chosen a mate, but they have disappointed you or failed your rather high standards, then the parting will be abrupt and final. The thing you hate most is being seen as a failure, and your love life is no exception. No gentle retreat for you, Capricorn, and your partner will certainly know in a very short time that it is all over for this romance.

Venus rules the sensual aspects of your character and shows that you do have a great deal of love and warmth to offer. Excitement and passion are an integral part of your personality, but only when the other person has proven their intrinsic worth and the relationship is running smoothly. You need to know that your life mate has a high level of commitment to the partnership before you will move to any next step.

When a mature Capricorn makes love, it is love-making at its very best. To a Capricorn there is no separation between love and sex, and you know by instinct when you have found the right partner for this immensely important ritual. For some people, sex is a release, a process of satisfying one of the basic needs in life. But Capricorns want to reach a state of total satisfaction, not only for themselves, but also for their partners, too.

The sign of Cancer rules your marriage affairs and to some extent your sexual feelings, so you can have a great relationship with this star sign. For you love and sex are intertwined with a sense of duty and, once you're sure your partner is your soulmate, you'll be openly playful in love.

Health, wellbeing and diet

You need to talk about how you feel, Capricorn, and not bottle up your emotions until it seems as though you will explode. This only causes tension for you and everyone around you. If you are not an active person it could cause emotional problems in your personal life. Show your feelings more readily and you'll less likely suffer stress-related disorders.

Most Capricorns always like to be doing something, even when they're relaxing. Combining television and a hobby such as knitting keeps a Capricorn busy and happy. However, you do need to listen to your body's signals so that you do not burn yourself out trying to do too many things at once.

Capricorns can suffer from rheumatism, bone disease, sterility, damage to their legs and knees, skin problems and depression. You need to get enough exercise, which, to a great degree, will help with any depression; but don't push yourself so hard that you damage bones, ligaments and tendons. Physical rigidity is associated with an inflexibility of the mind; the two go hand in hand.

Another area of weakness could be your lungs. By doing yoga and deep-breathing exercises, your body will be strengthened and meditation can also help keep you balanced.

Capricorn, you need a regular and balanced diet to keep you fit and well enough to maintain your desire for hard work. Skipping meals is going to lead to vitamin deficiencies, especially from the B group, the trade-off for which will be nervous irritability.

Your ruling planet Saturn is a slow-moving one and, in the evening when your metabolism is slow, don't make your last meal of the day the heaviest one. This will put an unwelcome load on your digestive system.

Soybean products, bean sprouts, eggs, wheat-germ and white meats, are all natural sources of the vitamins you need. Take a supplement if you're not eating enough natural foods.

Wholegrains and unprocessed foods are a great source of dietary nutrition for Capricorn. Acid-forming foods should be avoided because they are likely to aggravate any arthritic or rheumatic tendencies. Beer and coffee can also irritate these parts of your system and should be avoided.

To strengthen your sinews and tendons, especially if you are no longer a young person, take glucosamine sulphate to help rebuild some of that tissue. Some flaxseed added to your diet will improve your energy levels and is a great antioxidant, too.

Work

A Capricorn is indeed a hard worker and could be in danger of being regarded as a workaholic, such is their dedication. However, you do not see hard work as a problem. You enjoy it. You like to see a job well done because it rewards you with an enormous amount of satisfaction and professional pride.

Hard work fulfils you on so many levels and it suits a Capricorn to be their own boss. You are self-motivated and, if you must work under others, you will only see this as a stepping stone on the path to moving away into your own business.

With your organised mind you will do well in a career of law, teaching, mining or other research-oriented activities. You like your workplace to be comfortable, tidy and well-sorted; but not neces-sarily luxuriously appointed, because you see extravagance as a waste of money.

As an employee you may seem to be a bit of a mystery to your workmates because you don't necessarily blend readily with others. However, your colleagues trust that you do the job you are being paid to do well. You take your responsibilities very seriously and can keep complex operations moving smoothly.

Key to karma, spirituality and emotional balance

'I acquire' seems to be the primary, motivating catch phrase for Capricorn. You'll certainly become wealthy later in your life, given your drive to succeed. But your challenge in life is to balance this need for greater wealth and possessions with mental peace and happiness.

The other side of your life—which is the emotion of love—must not be neglected in the process. You will work hard for your family, to provide them with material things they need, but don't leave yourself out of the picture. The enjoyment of those home comforts you worked so hard for is just as important for your emotional wellbeing.

Achieving and keeping a balanced life could be quite a challenge for you, Capricorn. Taking time out for yourself may not initially appeal to your rather driven personality, but it is time well spent to keep you healthy in mind, body and spirit.

Your lucky days

Your luckiest days are Wednesdays, Fridays and Saturdays.

Your lucky numbers

Remember that the forecasts given later in the book will help you optimise your chances of winning. Your lucky numbers are:

8, 17, 26, 35, 44, 53

5, 14, 23, 32, 41, 50

6, 15, 24, 33, 42, 51

Your destiny years

Your most important years are 8, 17, 26, 35, 44, 53, 62, 71 and 80.

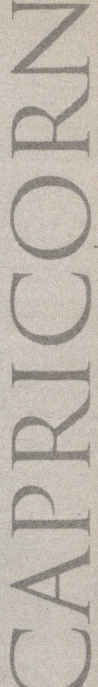

Star Sign
Compatibility

Love life and life will love you back. Love people and
they will love you back.

—Arthur Rubinstein

Romantic compatibility

How compatible are you with your current partner,
lover or friend? Did you know that astrology can
reveal a whole new level of understanding between
people simply by looking at their star sign and that
of their partner? In this chapter I'd like to share
some special insights that will help you better
appreciate your strengths and challenges using Sun
sign compatibility.

The Sun reflects your drive, willpower and
personality. The essential qualities of two star signs
blend like two pure colours, producing an entirely
new colour. Relationships, similarly, produce their
own emotional colours when two people interact.
The following is a general guide to your romantic
prospects with others and how, by knowing the
astrological 'colour' of each other, the art of love
can help you create a masterpiece.

When reading the following I ask you to remember
that no two star signs are ever *totally* incompatible.
With effort and compromise, even the most 'difficult'
astrological matches can work. Don't close your mind
to the full range of life's possibilities! Learning about
each other and ourselves is the most important facet
of astrology.

Each star sign combination is followed by the

elements of those star signs and the results of their combining. For instance, Aries is a fire sign and Aquarius is an air sign, and this combination produces a lot of 'hot air'. Air feeds fire and fire warms air. In fact, fire requires air. However, not all air and fire combinations work. I have included information about the different birth periods within each star sign and this will throw even more light on your prospects for a fulfilling love life with any star sign you choose.

Good luck in your search for love, and may the stars shine upon you in 2011!

Compatibility quick-reference guide

Each of the twelve star signs has a greater or lesser affinity with one another. The quick-reference guide will show you who's hot and who's not so hot as far as your relationships are concerned.

CAPRICORN + ARIES

Earth + Fire = Lava

Well, here we have the combination of Aries, which moves at a highly accelerated pace, with you, Capricorn, being sober, practical and steady. Either you will get left behind in the Aries' dust as they take off at their usual frenetic speed, or you will need to put your foot down hard on your own accelerator to keep up with them. These differences in attitude might explain why this relationship might be a little more difficult to maintain than many other star sign combinations.

Quick-reference guide: Horoscope compatibility between signs (percentage)

	Aries	Taurus	Gemini	Cancer	Leo	Virgo	Libra	Scorpio	Sagittarius	Capricorn	Aquarius	Pisces
Aries	60	65	65	65	90	45	70	80	90	50	55	65
Taurus	65	70	70	80	70	90	75	85	50	95	80	85
Gemini	70	70	75	60	80	75	90	60	75	50	90	50
Cancer	65	80	60	75	70	75	60	95	55	45	70	90
Leo	90	70	80	70	85	75	65	75	95	45	70	75
Virgo	45	90	75	75	75	70	80	85	70	95	50	70
Libra	70	75	90	60	65	80	80	85	80	85	95	70
Scorpio	80	85	60	95	75	85	85	90	80	65	60	50
Sagittarius	90	50	75	55	95	70	80	85	85	55	60	75
Capricorn	50	95	50	45	45	95	85	65	55	85	70	85
Aquarius	55	80	90	70	70	50	95	60	60	70	80	55
Pisces	65	85	50	90	75	70	50	95	75	85	55	80

You are certainly very different in the way you approach things. You, Capricorn, need a carefully mapped-out plan, a specific goal in mind, and also like to know exactly what you are doing. Aries, although also being somewhat goal orientated (but maybe not as much as you are), needs the thrill of the chase, spur of the moment decisions and likes to live more on the edge than you do. They will take risks you would not even consider.

Astrologically this combination can be quite challenging and romantically it is not the best of matches, either. It could even be argued that it is one of the less successful partnerships of the zodiac. However, in a business arena, this combination does have something going for it. There are opportunities for both of you to gain advantages by working together, even if you're not that similar in temperament on a romantic level. As a team you can certainly make money and gain many material benefits from this pairing.

You are introverted and shy, Capricorn, while Aries is quite up-beat and extroverted, and this is mainly due to your ruling planets of Saturn and Mars, respectively. Aries likes to call the shots, to organise things, and will feel devalued if you take this role away from them. Their fiery and boisterous energy needs scope for expression and they like to be the ones in charge. You can put out their rather bright Arian fire if you are too heavy handed or ponderous while getting things done.

Your nature is rather deliberate and slow, and you may find it difficult, if not impossible, to get your speed up to match the pace that Aries sets. They, on the other hand, will not react very well to your stern attitude and need to be given the freedom to get things done—and preferably done their way.

Aries born between the 21st and the 31st of March are fiery, rash and impatient characters who aren't very compatible with you in any area of life.

Aries born between the 1st and the 10th of April will be very frustrating for you. They are quite egocentric and don't take advice all that well. If you don't mind having a good argument, then you might consider a relationship with these people.

Aries born between the 11th and the 20th of April are ruled by Sagittarius and Jupiter. These people are larger-than-life characters who have big plans, like you, but their style is very different to yours. They are industrious and need to see results much more quickly than you do.

CAPRICORN + TAURUS
Earth + Earth = Solid Ground

You have a natural affinity with the matter-of-fact and earthy Taurus, because you see much of yourself reflected in them. You'll feel attracted to each other from the day you first meet and, when two earth signs team up like this, it makes for an excellent combination.

Taurus is just as security conscious as you are, Capricorn. You are also both traditional and dependable. Taurus will act as a solid backbone to you on all practical levels. You will develop a mutual respect for each other through these similarities. Another area in which you are alike is your ambitiousness, so you'll place a great deal of importance on achieving your worldly plans and goals together.

If you show your love to Taurus, you'll see that there's nothing they won't do in return to help you. By joining forces with them you will increase your chances of success. With your natural understanding of each other you'll be totally in sync in your daily routines.

You like to try new things, Capricorn, but Taurus is not so keen to do this. They find it hard to let go of the past, and any imposed change will only cause them to react. You first need to win their trust and this will be a significant issue between you. Your relationship can work over the long term, but initially this trust will need to be developed and almost carved in stone for the relationship to be a success.

At first Taurus may not understand your needs because you are a little more serious and withdrawn than they are. This particularly applies to your deep emotional and sexual desires. If you can't explain to them what it is that lights you up, how do you expect them to be able to even begin to fulfil your desires? You need to tell them! Taurus needs a demonstration of your affection and, if they don't receive it, they'll become dissatisfied.

There's a special connection between yourself and those Taureans born between the 21st and the 29th of April. They are very sensual, loving and attentive to your needs, with the influence of Venus. They'll make you feel loved and appreciated.

Trust is very important to them, so make sure that you are able to develop this early in the relationship. This will propel your relationship forward in a very satisfactory way for the both of you.

Taureans born between the 30th of April and the 10th of May are only moderately compatible with you. However, you can still expect many entertaining times and also be able to have a good laugh with them. They are quite humorous characters.

By far the most compatible group for you will be Taureans who are quite similar in nature to you and they will be born between the 11th and the 21st of May. They are co-ruled by your own ruler, Saturn. You'll readily get on well with them and they have similar material and financial goals, too. This could be a truly excellent relationship.

CAPRICORN + GEMINI
Earth + Air = Dust

You need to lighten up if you are going to succeed in a relationship with a Gemini, I'm afraid. They are airy-fairy, quite often scattered and not too keen on your Capricornian seriousness. The reason for this difference is that your element is earth and Gemini's is air. You may even stifle them if you are too heavy handed. However, your ruler, the slow and steady Saturn, is a redeeming factor in the relationship. Earth is scattered by air, and this is what may happen with a Gemini. They need variety while you need grounding.

Your sign falls in a very complicated area of the zodiac for Gemini, predominantly relating to assets and money. You need to make yourself quite clear about such issues and get Gemini to do the same. If you are not on the same page in this respect, there could be trouble in paradise, largely to do with finances.

You also need to talk through what it is you both want from the relationship. You as a Capricorn are interested in security, including financial security, whereas Gemini is less concerned with acquiring money and will spend it quite happily and generously. The colour may drain from your face, Capricorn, when you see your hard-earned dollars being spent on things you normally wouldn't dream of buying.

Although all relationships need to be based on some give and take, with this combination, the idea of you doing all the giving and Gemini doing all the taking doesn't sit too well with you at all. Actually, this could be so undesirable to you that it could be the rock on which the relationship flounders. If making money is your primary objective, consider that it could eventually have a negative effect on what could otherwise be a wonderful experience for you both.

However, Capricorn and Gemini can enjoy each other sexually. Gemini is playful and very stimulating, and this will help to unwind and relax you.

You have great focus and in this way would be able to help Gemini overcome their restlessness, giving them a direction in life and clarifying where they are going.

Geminis born between the 22nd of May and the 1st of June are wild and wacky and you may feel that you have signed on for a lifetime's worth of roller-coaster rides. It may be difficult to get your timetables to coincide because they might seem to be everywhere all at once, without rhyme or reason. The biggest challenge for you with this group will be to adjust your lifestyles so you can both be in the same place at the same time.

Your rapport with Geminis born between the 2nd and the 12th of June is special. You feel attracted to them and, of all the Geminis, these are the best suited to you. They can make you feel relaxed and happy. Even though they may sometimes come across as being a little highly strung, they have a tendency to know what to do and say at just the right time.

Those Geminis born between the 13th and the 21st of June will satisfy you if you have a leaning towards intellectual interests. They are mentally orientated and communication will be the focus of your relationship if you embark on a romance with them.

CAPRICORN + CANCER
Earth + Water = Mud

When you look at the signs of Capricorn and Cancer, there are quite a few differences, even though Cancer is your opposite sign. There is a saying that opposites attract, but your ruling planets of Saturn and the Moon, respectively, are very different in the way they express themselves. Because earth plus water equals mud, it is important you are clear in your expression at all times and don't let confusion rule your relationship with Cancer.

Cancers are able to express their feelings much more readily than you can, Capricorn. They are warm and demonstrative, but you may hold back in letting your feelings show until you feel fairly secure with them. A relationship with Cancer can be promising, but the emotional side of this combination must be completely transparent if it is to work.

Although Cancer, like you, wants emotional and domestic security, they are not as concerned as you are with the money and power side of it. This is at odds with your view on things. You love money and the way it opens doors for you towards material success, and you tend to identify emotionally with what you have in life.

Cancer sees it differently. They have a simpler and more intuitive way of living. Even though you're both traditional in your values, you see financial security as a critical ingredient for a happy and well-adjusted life. Cancer is very happy to have money, but what they need from you more is to feel nurtured and supported. Money itself will not be a deciding factor in whether or not they want to be in a relationship with you.

There needs to be clear definitions of what you both expect from this relationship. You, Capricorn, need to work harder at the emotional level and not let it become a form of barter because, on some level, this relationship is destined to be one of convenience.

Sexually your Sun signs are very different. Capricorn, you know how to give but you're just a little slow on the uptake and initially Cancer may find your affection to be slightly cooler than they would like it to be. Cancer must be patient and slowly educate you on what their needs are for this union to be a success in the bedroom.

Cancerians born between the 22nd of June and the 3rd of July are warm and sensitive. Emotionally they will nourish you and make you feel more open and giving in return. If you're looking for marriage with a Cancerian, you may do well with this group and it definitely deserves consideration.

You can experience great friendship with Cancerians whose birth dates fall between the 4th and the 13th of July. They are moody and tend to be volatile and angry if they don't get their own way. This could result in a clash of wills.

There is an attraction to Cancers born between the 14th and the 23rd of July, but it is likely to be more platonic than romantic. This group will trigger your spiritual aspirations.

CAPRICORN + LEO
Earth + Fire = Lava

Do you want someone who is the complete opposite to you? Then look no further. You two are poles apart in this combination; in how the Sun rules Leo and how it also rules Capricorn.

Leo loves to be in the limelight, but you don't want to spend time in the shadows, either, Capricorn, so there could be a bit of a power struggle for who is going to be the shining star between you. It may be worth your while to take a back seat occasionally and let Leo take centre stage, which is where they think they rightfully belong. If you keep your egos under control, this will not be a problem.

Leo is bright and zesty and can feel quite out of sorts if asked to be calm and deliberate, as you would like them to be. In matters of affection, another level of incompatibility is evident. Leos, with their fire element, are spontaneous and prepared to try new things; whereas you, Capricorn, are more traditional and habitual. To reach a happy medium you may both need to adjust a little.

Leo is impulsive, likes to improvise and entertain, whereas you're more comfortable hanging out in a relaxed environment. Your need for privacy will be at the opposite end of the spectrum from the social lifestyle to which Leo aspires.

The fire of Leo and your earthy nature are elements that do not connect easily and this is a fundamental difference in your star signs. Leo would need to develop sensitivity to your needs and stay up-beat if you take life too seriously so that there is balance in the relationship.

The sign of Leo falls into your area of loss and karmic debts. Both signs have a relevance to authority, power and control, so there may be something fated about your meeting with Leo. Even if it is not outwardly obvious, there is no doubt that you'll both be vying for control in this relationship.

In matters of intimacy, the basic differences in your expression are obvious and this is why your compatibility isn't so strong.

Take it easy with Leos born between the 24th of July and the 4th of August. They have a double-Sun influence and this will burn a hole through your cool demeanour, causing difficulties for both of you. There's very little similarity in your personalities, especially in the way you save or spend your money, an area that could cause daily problems.

Of the three types of Leo, you'll probably do better with someone born between the 5th and the 14th of August. They aren't as antagonistic as some of the other Leos. They are very optimistic and you'll appreciate their generosity and high ideals.

There's an antagonistic group of Leos born between the 15th and the 23rd of August. They are very highly motivated by you, but don't like being controlled. Don't even bother trying to tell them what to do. If you can bite your tongue, then you have a chance with one of these people.

CAPRICORN + VIRGO

Earth + Earth = Solid Ground

A rock-solid relationship can be formed with Virgo. You are two earth signs and, if you join forces, you have every chance of success. There is an immediate attraction between you. For some reason, Virgo does not find you quite as serious as some of the other signs do. This is probably because they are a fairly sober type of personality, too!

An example of a perfect combination is Humphrey Bogart and Lauren Bacall. On and off screen they were an ideal couple, both down to earth, and Bogart's ambitious nature would have inspired Bacall.

Virgo is a little more intellectual in style than you are, Capricorn, but they will uplift you and make you feel refreshed, young and responsive. Virgo, being ruled by Mercury, is also a little mischievous at times, and you can enjoy their spontaneous playfulness. You have serious and ambitious ways, but occasionally you can put these to one side and have a little fun.

The combination of Capricorn and Virgo can make a successful partnership in financial and practical matters as well. You can both work towards your material goals in a relaxed and conventional way.

You have a strong impact on the emotional life of Virgo. You are both amorous in each other's company and, even if Virgo is quite a critical sign and preoccupied with details, they won't seem to be quite so compelled to burden you with their views of your character traits.

A similarity in the workplace is that you are both reasonably methodical, give great store to attention to detail and can be trusted to work alone and at your own pace. You trust each other and feel confident working in each other's company, so there could be a sensitive and loving relationship there for you.

Virgo can give you the long-term security that you're looking for, Capricorn. You'll both find it easy to express your love and make each other feel secure and comfortable.

Virgos born between the 24th of August and the 2nd of September are spiritually orientated and can teach you many things. They can influence your mental development and you may have the opportunity to meet Virgo in some sort of study course. Another way you may meet is through some teaching, legal or advisory work.

If you're looking for love, those Virgos born between the 3rd and the 12th of September are perfectly aligned with you. You have much in common with them because Saturn also co-rules their star sign. You can be optimistic about the future with them.

You're attracted to Virgos born between the 13th and the 23rd of September. Venus makes them amorous, so therefore love, pleasure and your social life will be activated by coming together.

CAPRICORN + LIBRA

Earth + Air = Dust

It is a necessary part of the process to get to know Libra before arriving at any conclusions, because you may be pleasantly surprised at how promising this match could be. A relationship between Capricorn and Libra can be quite a good one, perhaps even resulting in marriage, so this combination is certainly worth considering.

Capricorn and Libra are ruled by Saturn and Venus, two of the friendliest planets in the zodiac. If you can overcome your desire to control Libra, the relationship will fare well. This is because, as you may well know, Capricorn, you have a driving need to direct a relationship, which will not sit too well with Libra. If you want a relationship that will fulfil both of you romantically, you need to overcome the idea of being the one at the helm.

Libra is much more concerned with balance than you are, Capricorn, and believes that sharing resources is the way to benefit everybody. You on the other hand aim for material success and the professional leverage it brings with it. There's a marked difference between you on this matter.

While you need to have possessions as a sign of your success, Libra needs people because they are more of a social sign. You're quite comfortable in your own company and don't go out of your way to have people fill up your life during any spare time you may have left over at the end of a working day. As a couple this attitude could present some challenges over the long term.

Whereas your driving force and reason for working is to accumulate money, Libra does not feel as strongly about this way of life, although they do enjoy the style, culture and finer things in life that can be provided for them. It will be only a small step to convince them that money, and what it can do, is quite desirable.

Work and pleasure combine well if you team up with Librans born between the 23rd September and 3rd October. There's a powerful influence of Venus with this group, making them sensual and demonstrative but, they will also support your professional efforts as well. It won't take them too much effort to win your heart.

Librans born between the 4th and the 13th of October will energise you and make you feel very stimulated. While in their company, you will notice they have a progressive streak to their personality, which makes them fun and quirky to be around. If you're prepared to try new things, then this relationship will be a good one in which you will learn much about each other.

The group of Librans born between the 14th and the 23rd of October have an important role to play in the development of your personality. They will shake up and loosen your conservative views, and overcoming your fear about doing this will be one of the best things you can look forward to with them. They are young at heart and will remind you of your own youth, helping to transform the serious side of your personality.

CAPRICORN + SCORPIO

Earth + Water = Mud

If you are looking for a good friend who can also be a lover, then Scorpio is an ideal match for you, Capricorn. Because Scorpio is a water sign, they tend to bring out your softer, emotional side. This will make you attracted to a relationship where you feel totally in tune with your partner. You instinctively feel Scorpios have your best interests at heart and have more depth to them than the average person.

Although your ruling planets aren't the best of friends, you do feel comfortable together, even early on in your relationship. Just as you are hard working, so too is Scorpio, who is ambitious as well. They set themselves goals and go after them with great determination. Scorpio is a more emotional sign than your own practical one. They also like power and the leverage it can offer them, whereas your driving force seems to be what money can buy.

You can have a very rewarding relationship with a Scorpio because they can also focus on the job at hand. As a combination you can amass wealth and power if you join forces.

If you choose to work and play together then balance is necessary in this relationship because power conflicts are likely to arise. Would you expect anything else with two such powerful signs joining forces? What a formidable duo you can be.

Your ruling planet Saturn is cool and detached, whereas Scorpio likes to express their sexuality in every possible way. On one level you are sexually compatible, but on another are quite different. Scorpio could quite overwhelm you at your first meeting, because you need time to warm to their advances. Their sexual enthusiasm may lead you to believe they have some sort of ulterior motive behind their behaviour. However, don't let an initial mistrust get in the way of a deeply fulfilling relationship.

You can expect a great friendship to develop with Scorpios born between the 24th of October and the 2nd of November. Although friendship is at the heart of this relationship, you will be amazed at the connection between you. There will be lots of friendly debate and discussion because you won't always agree on everything.

If you want a partner with whom you can have some great times, then consider Scorpios born between the 3rd and the 12th of November. They see your compassionate and generous side, which naturally draws them into a relationship with you. They have the intuitive influence of Pisces, so sometimes they will appear to have their head in the clouds rather than being tuned into you. You will soon find they actually do have their feet on the ground most of the time, and that they are loving and caring individuals.

If you're involved with a Scorpio born between the 13th and the 22nd of November, this is quite an achievement in itself. This group of Scorpios is one of the most challenging of the zodiac; however, they are the best match for you out of this star sign. Your relationship will deepen very quickly with them because they have the Moon's influence on them.

CAPRICORN + SAGITTARIUS

Fire + Earth = Lava

From the outset you will be attracted to Sagittarius, with their outgoing temperament and warm, robust personalities. Although you're really quite different from each other, there's an alluring quality about Sagittarius that makes them quite difficult to resist. Saturn rules your character and therefore your personality is likely to be inward looking and detached. However, once you are involved with a Sagittarian, all this will change.

Capricorn has a more conservative approach than Sagittarius and can appear to be a little on the pessimistic side when compared to the enthusiasm and optimism of Sagittarius. You may feel a little unsettled by them but will eventually become more comfortable in their company because their jovial personality and easygoing lifestyle is in stark contrast to your own approach.

Sagittarians have a love of adventure and freedom, often enjoying dangerous sports, whereas Capricorn does not share this trait, being far more cautious. If you team up with a Sagittarian you would need to accept this drive as part and parcel of their personality, even though you may not necessarily want to go along for the ride on their adventures.

Sagittarians like spending money, whereas you like saving it. If you take the time to give Sagittarius more information on money matters, it may be possible for you to find a happy balance to make your financial life work harmoniously for both of you.

Fire is a warm and nourishing element, and this will have a tonic effect on your character, stimulating you to explore life with your Sagittarian partner. Hopefully Sagittarius will see the value of spending more time with you, because at first your rather less-than-effervescent personality will leave them high and dry.

As far as your sexual chemistry with Sagittarius is concerned, you both need time to explore what satisfies you. Initially it is not likely to be a hot, heavy and passionate affair, but if you try hard to respond and aren't too reserved with them, this should help fan the flames and keep the romance alive. Drop the traditional attitudes for a while and you'll find yourself learning and progressing so much more.

There's a good opportunity for a meaningful relationship with Sagittarians born between the 23rd of November and the 1st of December. They are less fiery and far more compatible with you, Capricorn. It's worth investing a bit of time to find out what makes them tick before committing yourself. You will be surprised at what you find.

Connecting with Sagittarians born between the 2nd and the 11th of December means you have to be prepared for a clash of personalities. They have strong egos and like to be right at all times and at all costs. This could have you pulling your hair out!

A relationship with Sagittarians born between the 12th and the 22nd of December can be quite difficult. It's hard to say exactly why this is, but there is just an air of general discomfort in this match. Take it slowly with them because your compatibility with them is not exactly first class.

CAPRICORN + CAPRICORN
Earth + Earth = Solid Ground

Here we have a rather formidable force, made up of the combined drive of two ambitious star signs. If you do happen to meet your star twin, you can expect success and bucket loads of financial benefits to come your way. By combining your creative forces you will enhance your power individually and as a couple.

There will be a stream of money coming to you both, which will in turn bring you luxuries and a more than comfortable lifestyle. You both have an instinctive feel for money, so if your partner is the same star sign and has these talents, too, it will make it easier for you to pool your resources and work together with a common goal.

However, financial and material interests are not the only things that drive you, Capricorn, even though up to now I have focused on them. It is more a matter of security that is at the heart of what motivates you; however, truly evolved Capricorns are able to work in the service of others quite happily. They will apply themselves to helping those less fortunate and aren't necessarily selfish.

Developing your inner wealth of emotional contentment will be much easier with your Capricorn star twin. Working with and loving another Capricorn will present all sorts of opportunities, financially and materially, as these things are the dominating influences on both of you.

You are both private people who like to spend time alone for lengthy periods. You and your Capricorn partner will appreciate the mood of quiet, restful and rejuvenating times at a mountain retreat or deserted beach. You will regularly need to get away from the hustle and bustle of modern business life and the demands it places on your time.

You are both workaholics and sometimes your ambitions and business and personal goals may take over your life to such an extent that you forget there is life outside of work. 'Work to live, not live to work,' could be just the motto for you, Capricorn. Remain sensitive enough to realise that for love to grow you have to make time for it and put some effort in.

Capricorns don't believe that lovemaking has to be a fireworks display each and every time. You're conservative in lovemaking, but your attitudes are so similar that this will not be a problem for you. To have a partner who is there for you when you need them and on whom you can totally rely is a real turn on for you, Capricorn. A stable and supportive relationship really lights you up and in time you start to feel more sexually comfortable in each other's company.

Generally, most Capricorns get on well with each other. Capricorns born between the 23rd of December and the 1st of January will make you feel very happy and are better suited to Capricorns born between the 2nd and the 10th of January. The combined influence of Saturn and Venus means your affection will grow and you have a natural affinity.

Combinations within the group of Capricorns born between the 11th and the 20th of January, like most others, will also be quite happy because of their extremely charming personalities. You'll relax and feel mentally stimulated when in each other's company.

CAPRICORN + AQUARIUS
Earth + Air = Dust

The combination of Capricorn and Aquarius is an unusual one, although you're both ruled by the same planet, Saturn. Aquarius is mostly swayed by the modern rulership of Uranus, the unpredictable and electric planet. On the other hand, Saturn is a stable and predictable planet, so at first the similarities between Capricorn and Aquarius might not be all that obvious and can elude you for some time, unless you're prepared to dig a little deeper into the relationship.

Aquarius believes that convention should be used as a guidepost for what can be broken down and then rebuilt anew. You, on the other hand, Capricorn, are motivated by traditional values, the tried and tested, and prefer walking along the well beaten track. Aquarians are not at all content to remain stationary or live in the past and much prefer to push themselves beyond their limits, and yours, too. Life to them is something to be explored and experienced. They have a rather experimental approach to the way they live their lives. I am sure you can see by now that this will be a challenge for you.

At times you'll believe these opposites can work well for you. Perhaps you and Aquarius are simply two sides of the same coin? To get you out of your comfort zone, you need a bit of a push or shove, whereas Aquarius will use your steady hand to keep them anchored in the here and now, in the real world. A relationship with Aquarius certainly won't be guaranteed to be secure and steady and your sensible nature may have trouble coming to terms with this difference in attitudes.

There are similarities in taste, with you both liking antiques and traditional art. But then, Aquarius also likes modern furnishings and abstract paintings. These same differences also exist in terms of your musical tastes and your general style.

Your sexual life may not be all that fulfilling for either of you. Aquarius likes to explore and take sex to a new level, which will possibly mean they see you as a little old-fashioned in your approach. This is not quite true because you're more than happy to try things, but you need time to warm to the idea and see what sexual opportunities are available to you before rushing headlong into it. If you could convince Aquarius to be a little more patient, this could bring you together in an even more intimate way than you had first imagined.

Aquarians born between the 21st and the 30th of January are the revolutionaries of the zodiac and will make you feel a little uneasy, especially if they want to move things too quickly for your taste.

Those born between the 31st of January and the 8th of February will bring joy and humour to the lives of many Capricorns, but they are not necessarily favoured for a long-term relationship with you.

You're comfortable, both intellectually and physically, with Aquarians born between the 9th and the 19th of February. Because Venus infuses their personalities with love and good taste, you can easily be drawn into a long-term relationship with them. At times they are a little excessive by nature and demand more affection and attention than you're able to give them, but otherwise, this could be a good match.

CAPRICORN + PISCES
Earth + Water= Mud

Good friendship is on the cards when Capricorn and Pisces meet. Generally, the idealistic Pisces and practical Capricorn are poles apart. Pisces isn't at all motivated by self-interest but by a sense of self-sacrifice. This is a bit hard for you to comprehend because you're so concrete and goal orientated. You like anything that can be proved and don't have much time for airy-fairy concepts. This is how you will see Pisces.

However, there are similarities in your basic temperament, with the feminine signs of Capricorn and Pisces both being considered intuitive and emotional, but more so for Pisces. It may actually surprise you, Capricorn, to realise how intuitive you are and it can work for you if you allow this hidden part of your temperament to be expressed. Pisces can naturally draw this out of you.

Pisces are daydreamers, often thinking with their hearts rather than their heads. This can be frustrating for you when you occasionally catch them off guard and you might misinterpret their idealism as simple impracticality. They do say that opposites attract, so here's your chance to prove the theory.

You, Capricorn, have a great capacity for sustained work and self-sacrifice, with a materialistic bent of mind. Pisces are selfless workers and like to exert themselves for the benefit of others. This will be an extremely good combination when both of you understand a little more about each other's motivations.

To bridge the gap, you could become less self-centred and driven by work, Capricorn. By involving Pisces in what you do, they will become more practical. Therefore, some good results can be obtained by teaming up with them and, although you're not entirely compatible, you'll feel comfortable working together. You may even be able to grow your relationship into something more solid and enduring.

Those Pisces born between the 20th and the 29th of February are extremely idealistic. You may have a great deal of difficulty with these people, and I doubt you will have a strong connection with them. However, consider that your judgement could be based on an initial, superficial impression, so try a little harder and don't judge them on your first meeting.

Pisces born between the 1st and the 10th of March have a strong Moon influence. This can make them moody; but nevertheless you will still feel comfortable with them and quite strongly connected. This match would make a good long-term partnership.

With Pisceans born between the 11th and the 20th of March, a great friendship is predicted. These are quite intense Pisceans, but they are much softer and more fragile than they first appear. Your sexual connectivity is not as strong but you should be able to enjoy their social companionship. This match is more likely to be a friendship than a hot and spicy affair.

2011:
The Year Ahead

Live your life and forget your age.

—Norman Vincent Peale

Romance and friendship

You are just now seeing the light at the end of the romantic tunnel, so to speak, Capricorn. The year 2011 is an exciting one in which romance can take you into new and uncharted territory. It could initially be a struggle, when your ruling planet distracts you with loads of work and other heavy responsibilities, but you do now have the opportunity to turn over a new leaf, begin afresh and enjoy love once again.

You're fortunate to have Venus and the Moon moving through your zone of friendship in January. You are keen to meet new people and take your friendships to a new level. This will also include increasing your sphere of social influence. These planets tend to fulfil your life's desire by bringing you in contact with a whole lot of new people who can make you feel good about yourself, and vice versa.

When Jupiter moves into your zone of family on the 11th of February, your home life will take on a new flavour and you will be keen to increase your time with loved ones and relatives. This planetary transit also has a great deal to do with real estate, property and issues surrounding your locality. It's a great time to look for a new house if you've been in a rut in your current residence.

Simply for the sake of seeing what is out there, you could find yourself at property auctions, looking at real estate and generally getting an idea of what alternatives are available to your current living circumstances. Even if you don't actually move, you will most certainly want to beautify your home and expand your living space. This will involve considerable renovation or other interior design activities. Just don't bite off more than you can chew.

March is a very significant month for developing your mental and communications techniques. This will serve to better your relationship prospects—whether new or existing. The secret of any good romance and marriage, in particular, is how well you can communicate with your partner. Fortunately you will be doing many things to improve this aspect of your personality. You will be studying, attending self-help groups and taking more of an interest in psychology and philosophy, etcetera.

At the end of the month, when Venus enters your zone of communication and travel, you will turn into a social butterfly and be able to implement some of these newly learned techniques. This will be an exciting phase and one that will bring you into a whole new set of experiences.

Tread warily throughout April because Mars, the contentious planet, brings strife into your personal affairs. Try not to push your views onto others, above all close members of the family. You may find someone as strong-willed as yourself opposing everything you wish to do. Yielding is probably the best way to resolve this issue for the moment, to keep the peace within your family circle.

Venus provides you with ample charm and the ability to get your ideas across in a simple and effective way. Try to be softly persuasive because, around this time, Mercury challenges you. Say a little less and slow down your speech. You will be impulsive and trying to impress others, but could end up doing the reverse. 'Silence is golden' and will serve you well if you are trying to make any new friendship.

At the end of April the Sun enters your zone of romance, so you can expect another cycle of upliftment in your creative and emotional lives. You will want to express yourself and need someone capable of sharing your feelings and reciprocating love. If this is not possible you would be best to generate and redirect these creative and loving energies into a hobby or other pastime, which will help you bypass some of the frustration that is possible if you don't have a partner.

At this time Venus endows you with sentimentality and you will reconnect with family members or friends from your past. You'll be in the mood to create harmony and, if anyone tries to interfere with this desire, you are likely to walk out and disappear for a while rather than confronting them with an argument.

The month of May must surely be one of the more important periods of the year, as Mercury,

Venus and Mars all jointly enter your zone of romance. This is a powerful combination, affecting both romance and lust. You will need inner strength and discipline to contain yourself and there's every possibility you will be challenged if you meet someone new. Passion could turn into anger if you are not careful.

This could also have something to do with the difficult aspect between Venus and the Sun. The result is that you could find yourself at odds with someone's philosophical or cultural differences. Finding a common meeting ground will be the challenge for you. If you compromise and the other person does the same, there's every chance your relationship will work out. Try to stand in the other person's shoes for a moment.

The planet Uranus is sudden in its action. When it impacts upon your family scene in June, get ready for some earth-shattering consequences in your family life. Relatives will come and go, and gossip and other unsavoury topics may be the highlight of your interactions within the family arena. You might find yourself having to justify why you are embroiled in the nitty-gritty of everyone else's problems. However, my suggestion is to stay clear of other people's business and keep to your own affairs.

Your sense of security could be ruffled as well. It is critical that you don't sweep these issues under the rug entirely. If you're feeling unsettled in any way, you mustn't allow others to coerce or emotionally manipulate you into making decisions you are not comfortable with. This is, in fact, a good time to settle into yourself and wait for the universe to give you some of the important answers to the questions you are asking.

You mustn't be too proud to accept an offer of help throughout July. Older people with more experience can shed light on your relationships and give you vital keys to unravelling the mystery of love and romance. High on your list of priorities is your most meaningful relationship and, if you're married, it will relate to some important changes that need to be implemented if you are to maintain happiness and harmony for the long term.

Contracts may also come under scrutiny, but these are not necessarily written contracts. If you've given your word, or someone else has offered assurances, then these issues could be under the microscope for inspection. Issues of trust will also now be very noteworthy.

Try not to be too concerned by what people think of you at this time. You need to feel comfortable in your own skin; wear clothes that befit your temperament, lifestyle and comfort level. It could be that you're trying to impress others and want to fit in with them, which will cause you to dress or act in ways that are completely inappropriate or out of character. Be true to yourself. People will appreciate you much more.

Jupiter, the planet of luck and good fortune, strongly affects your zone of romance between June and August. You'll experience a better state of affairs in your love life. Although Jupiter is not particularly friendly to your Sun sign, it is still considered a first-rate benefactor, offering you the hope of improved romantic conditions. You may meet someone who is caring, kind and generous in disposition.

They will also make you feel good by lifting your spirits and possibly even introducing you to some spiritual activities that will broaden your self-awareness and self-confidence. Sexual issues will also be spotlighted throughout this month and you can expect a great deal of enjoyment in this area of your life.

In September and October unfinished business with a parent can be finally concluded. There's no point holding grudges against anyone anymore, especially those who are so close to your heart. Resolve issues, and make forgiveness your key word. It will allow you to complete 2011 with a clear conscience and better sense of self.

In the concluding part of the year, November and December, expect an amplification of your social activities. You'll be placing more importance on friendships, group activities and goals that you generally wish to achieve in life. Be careful, however, of getting embroiled in secret liaisons with people who can't possibly offer you a fulfilling future. You must fight for what you believe in, and under no circumstances, compromise your moral or ethical principles.

In December, leading up to Christmas, it's time for making peace, letting go of the past and extending your hand in friendship and forgiveness. By looking forward to the future and not brooding over what has been, you stand the best chance of not only personal success and liberation, but deep satisfaction in your loving relationships as well.

Work and money

In 2011 your financial, career and business activities are dominated by Saturn, your ruling planet. Its transit through the upper part of your horoscope is testimony to the strong responsibilities you have to shoulder. Notwithstanding these duties, Saturn, being in its favourite sign of Libra, is an excellent omen for success and a positive outcome.

Throughout January, Mars and the Sun combine to provide energy and determination, thereby propelling you towards your goals in the coming year. You're not afraid to meet challenges head-on and, as a result of Venus's excellent aspect to your career zone, you will find yourself in the good books with your superiors. You will enjoy your responsibilities and thrive on the pressures of work.

Set clear parameters for your work colleagues in the early part of the year, because your style may be cramped by others. Let them know exactly how you want your work to be conducted. You need to assume a leadership role so there are no misunderstandings.

You are fired up to earn money throughout February, due to Mars in your zone of finance. But this may also produce some impulsive spending that could, in turn, result in disputes with others. Talk about these issues before you go on big spending sprees.

In February and March you are challenged in your work life. Irrespective of whether you're a professional or a home-maker, you may find some of the sheen wearing off the joy that you enjoyed in the first month of the year. It could be that you're overdoing it. Make time to rest and enjoy some pleasure as well.

You have the opportunity to study and increase your knowledge throughout March. Learn more about your job, increase your skills, and don't be afraid to ask others their advice so that you can become better at what you do. Someone close to you may be the catalyst for you becoming a student once again.

Contractual arrangements are rather dicey, when Mars activates your zone of agreements during this same time frame. Think carefully before signing on the dotted line, and don't commit yourself to anything impulsively. You will regret it. You will also find your environment noisy or cluttered and this will impact adversely on your work. Get away from co-workers if they impede your progress.

You are torn between family and obligations to work. Divided loyalties cause you restlessness and even poor sleep patterns. Balance these important areas of your life throughout April, otherwise you may do neither well. Feeling under pressure, you will say and do things you regret and this again is due to the impact of the quick-tempered Mars.

Throughout May, Saturn is challenged by almost all of the planets in your zone of family. The issue mentioned above will continue for some time as you determine what it is you really want out of life. This is also a cycle in which you need to dig deeply to see whether or not your work is giving you the satisfaction you truly seek. If you are not happy, get out and do something you love, irrespective of your age. The universe will support you.

Flashes of inspiration, yet also moments of complete surprise, could punctuate your working life in June and July. The planet Uranus will spur you on to more independent thinking and action, which could cause you suddenly to leave a job you have done for many years. This may seem exciting to some of you; but remember, you are a Capricorn and impulsiveness is not one of your most notable character traits. Think carefully before embarking on a new path.

In July, August and September you'll have an avid interest in finances or negotiating the terms of your banking, superannuation, investments and other long-term planning strategies. You will need to think outside the square to create the best outcomes for yourself. Travelling and doing business with people at a distance is also favoured throughout the same time frame. Connecting finances with foreign activities is advisable.

In October and November you can look forward to excellent profits thanks to the advice and assistance of friends who are looking out for your best interests. There is a quick turnover in business due to the influence of Mercury and Venus on your zone of business income. Make sure you remain aboveboard in your dealings, especially if you're in a business partnership, because a contentious issue rears its ugly head again.

In the last part of the year there could be some frustrations in your work when the Sun challenges your career zone. Mars also has an impact on legal matters and therefore you should try to resolve differences of opinion and legal or financial matters with all concerned before Christmas. This way you'll enjoy the benefits of the festive season without the stress of work.

Overall, the outcome for 2011 is excellent, with the final transit of Venus in your zone of finance, adding a positive spin to your monetary affairs.

Karma, luck and meditation

The year 2011 is an important one for your karma. With your ruling planet transiting its most favourable sign of Libra, this is an auspicious period in which your hard work pays off. Your persistence, diligence and high degree of concentration is what will create continued luck for you in the coming twelve months; not just emotionally, but in other areas of your life as well.

The positive karmic planets for Capricorn are most notably Venus and Mercury. There is a tug of war between your instincts to earn a lot of money, to capitalise on friendships and good connections, but to also extend yourself in the areas of compassionate work by helping those less fortunate than yourself, and generally portraying a more caring and spiritual demeanour to the outside world.

The key periods for you in the coming twelve months are February, May, June, July, September and October. In these months, Venus, your most prominent karmic planet, will bring excellent results in romance, finance, marriage, travel and career.

In particular, the transit of Venus is very telling on your spiritual evolution, because the upper part of your horoscope brings your past good deeds to fruition. Don't for a minute think that the present good luck in your life is some sort of accident.

Wonderful romantic and relationship energy is forecast for you when Mercury, the Sun and the Moon transit your zone of marriage in the early part of July. You can look forward to some wonderful romantic interludes at this time.

Your past good actions will now reap great results and you are poised to enjoy them throughout 2011.

Your Bonus 2010 Three Month Forecast

Highlights of the month

The enthusiasm, vitality and passion from you that I discussed in September continues during October and the two planets, Venus and Mars, edge their way together through your zone of friendships and life fulfilment. If you've been sensing someone's attraction for you, you're probably correct.

Between the 1st and the 4th, Cupid's arrows may hit you directly in the heart—bullseye! But you mustn't be shy or doubtful about someone's intentions. If your intuition whispers in your ear that you have a good shot at love, at romance, then open your heart to the range of human possibilities and accept the invitation. This is no time to be playing mind games.

There could be some divided loyalties this month with an additional pair of planets, the Sun and Saturn, dominating the upper part of your horoscope that represents your career, employment and commitment. Around the 8th there may even be opportunities to 'ascend the throne'.

A promotion is likely but this could be received reluctantly because you realise an additional amount of time and effort will be required to fulfil the role. If you foresee yourself in a situation that won't make you feel happy, it's best to decline and not let your ego get the better of you.

Sudden flashes of luck and inspiration punctuate your affairs between the 10th and 17th, and you have Jupiter and Uranus to thank for that, being placed in your third zone of communication. But also, unknown to many, even to astrologers, this third house is lucky for lottery tickets, raffles and other games of chance.

With Venus and Mars also influencing the fifth zone of speculation, I daresay it would be worth taking a punt this month, especially between the 18th and the 24th. Who knows? You may just get lucky and find yourself the recipient of some additional cash or at least a hamper at the local club.

Your mental state has to be perfectly in tune with your bodily state from the 25th till the 27th. If you are hell-bent on doing something great in life, it will be wasted if your convictions aren't true. Why are you doing what you do? Is it to impress someone? Is it for glory and adulation? Or do you genuinely love what you are doing? If love is your motive, you're on the right path.

When Mars finally moves into your zone of secrets, hospitals and hidden activities on the 28th, you may need to extend yourself and show some compassion to someone who needs help. Make yourself available because the outcome of this is a wonderful sense of relief and spiritual upliftment for having participated. The key word in the last couple of days of the month is 'selflessness'.

Romance and friendship

You don't want to come across as too serious between the 1st and the 7th but, by the same token, you don't want others to take advantage of you. There could be a sense of growing responsibility and maturity about you during this first part of October and you could be giving off the wrong signals to others. Instead, you could use others as a form of marketing to spread the message out about how you feel and who you really are. Talk to a few close friends whom you know have big mouths and this will spread the word!

Venus and Mars again combine forces in your zone of friendships this month and things can hot up in this arena. Use their power to enjoy your life, make some new friends and even enjoy the spontaneous passion of the moment. By the time Mercury conjoins Saturn around the 8th, you could be feeling less communicative and may want others to do more of the talking.

Between the 10th and the 14th, a jam-packed social agenda is forecast. You could be rather anxious about how others will perceive you but your worst enemy is your own fear. Hold up your head and be yourself.

The new Moon around the 16th is an excellent omen for putting your best foot forward in relationships. You mustn't let the past encroach upon the way you deal with others. Someone you used to be involved with may come out of the woodwork and make you feel nervous. Use your unconventional wisdom to sidestep this encounter and continue to enjoy the situation.

Between the 28th and the 30th, you could find yourself in a compromising situation. If you've agreed to help someone to do something or be somewhere that eventually turns out to embarrassing, it will be hard to extricate yourself from it. A little bit of research and investigation beforehand might give you the 'heads up' before it's too late.

Work and money

You might be placing way too much emphasis on your earning capacity rather than your capacity to love what you do. Take some time to reconsider your direction between the 3rd and the 7th. You could well be making money but at the expense of your inner peace and creative satisfaction.

Venus, the planet ruling your career zone, moves into retrograde motion on the 8th and this indicates important changes could take place with respect to your career or workplace agreements. Being fore-warned, you are forearmed, and need to take the necessary measures to avoid problems. Get proactive if you see something wrong, even if it involves your employer. Speak up but do it in a way that is not offensive.

The clever communications occurring between the 18th and the 25th open new doorways of opportunities for you. New contacts can help you achieve a coveted position by way of an introduction around the 26th. A quick change of plans after the 28th will be necessary to keep up with changing times.

Destiny dates

Positive: 15, 16, 17, 18, 19, 20, 21, 22, 23, 24, 25, 26, 27

Negative: 8, 29, 30

Mixed: 1, 2, 3, 4, 5, 6, 7, 8, 10, 11, 12, 13, 14, 28

NOVEMBER 2010

Highlights of the month

Whatever confusion you've had regarding money will be cleared up, much to your satisfaction, between the 1st and the 4th. What's more, you'll find yourself the recipient of increased cash flow just when you need it, leading up to Christmas. Mercury, Venus and the Sun give you several opportunities or streams of income from which to draw upon, due to their presence in your zone of profitability.

The Moon also is not a bad omen, commencing its transit this month in your zone of fortune, luck and karma. This indicates that some of your good karma is ripening and likely to come back to you in the form of cold, hard cash, especially between the 5th and the 7th.

Venus on the 8th moves back into your professional zone, your area of self-esteem and your ego, indicating a boost to your public persona and the way others see you. You may choose to change your wardrobe, enhance your elegance and make others take note of you for who you are, not so much for what you do. You're still likely to do good work, and to bring to your activities a touch of style and creativity, for which Venus is well known.

Artistic pursuits seem to be high on your 'to do' list and you mustn't avoid going to that concert or art exhibition, or you yourself participating in some sort of creative or craft hobby. These things will help soothe your mind and give you a much-needed boost in energy, especially after the 16th.

Between the 19th and the 22nd it's 'all systems go', for a new relationship or friendship that previously you felt may have stalled. You might have given up on someone who took your phone number and didn't bother to call you in the first few days. But, much to your surprise, that long-awaited call may indeed come!

Hold onto your money and your personal belongings around the 23rd. Pay special attention to where you leave your valuables and, if possible, lock them away, especially if you have guests coming over whom you've not been familiar with before. Attention to detail is again an important aspect of short-circuiting losses and other financial problems.

The month ends with the return of Venus to your zone of friendship and fulfilment. Superb romantic opportunities take place on the 30th. You'll be feeling happy in your friendships and discussions you have with someone, which could make you feel very special.

Some of your personal goals may be highlighted at this time. If you've had a hobby or a creative pastime that you haven't had much time for lately, this is an excellent period in which to recommit yourself to the path of beauty and artistic excellence.

Romance and friendship

A well-earned rest is quite likely to be the order of the day between the 1st and the 4th. You owe it to yourself to take some time out, especially if you've been bending over backwards to satisfy everyone else.

You feel sentimental between the 5th and the 7th but may not have that sentimentality reciprocated. As a result, you may need to put on a false face just to handle the situation. Don't let frustrations build up. You need to speak about how you feel.

You have a strong desire for travel, exploration and adventure between the 8th and the 11th. You could find yourself 'between a rock and a hard place' if your friend or partner is not in the same mood. Who said you can't travel alone? Are you adventurous enough to do it independently, is the question.

Many unresolved matters can come to a head around the 19th, with Jupiter and Venus giving you great energy to clear up confusions. On the same day, the Moon will make you emotional and able to take control of the situation without being too aggressive about it.

Don't be afraid to call for help between the 22nd and the 28th. Others are more than happy to help you understand your situation, especially if they have more experience in a certain area than you do. A wounded pride could be what's stopping you from reaching out to them. On the 30th, you'll be pleased to note someone extending their hand in friendship to reciprocate.

This is a month for resolving differences and for acting upon your own self-beliefs.

Work and money

You can manifest your visions at work after the 8th. This is an excellent time to use the powers of persuasion, your charm and other social skills to convince others of your suitability for a job or project. Behind-the-scenes activities, secret collaborations, rumour mongering and other subversive activities between the 9th and the 14th, strangely assist you in gaining a coveted position. This could involve a certain amount of undercover work to get the information you need.

If you are reckless with your wealth, you will quickly lose it, particularly between the 14th and the 21st. Make sure you've accounted for your money by keeping all your receipts, because it may be too late when you forget where and with whom you transacted.

Don't overlook an important principle in business—or friendships, for that matter—and that is to say thank you when someone does you a favour. People could be forgiven for feeling as if you are using them as a means to an end if you don't show some appreciation for the contacts and business that they swing your way. This is likely to be an oversight on your part around the 26th or 27th.

Destiny dates

Positive: 1, 2, 3, 4, 5, 6, 7, 30
Negative: 9, 10, 11, 14, 15, 16, 17, 18
Mixed: 8, 19, 20, 21, 22, 23, 24, 25, 26, 27, 28

DECEMBER 2010

Highlights of the month

On the 6th Uranus, the planet of innovation, foresight and abrupt but exciting events, moves forward and tells us that December is going to be anything but boring for you!

You are highly strung, edgy, but also able to contain your feelings and direct your energies into traditional and practical pathways to achieve a considerable amount leading up to Christmas. Mostly due to the positioning of the Sun and Mars in the quiet area of your horoscope, you should be able to do much of your work behind the scenes, especially in the first week of the month.

Between the 10th and the 14th, you can come out of your shell and blast apart any opposition to your plans, whether on the home front or in the workplace. Expect others to question your motivation but my suggestion for you is to stick to your guns. If you know you're right due to the huge amount of research that you've done on something, plough through it like a steamer through ice, and don't look back!

There may be some problems with people who want to undermine you throughout December and so you can expect the odd rumour or piece of gossip to head your way. Pay no attention to it and keep on working hard, up until the lunar eclipse on the 21st, which occurs in your zone of work and service. The truth will be revealed at this time, and you'll be vindicated. Silence is golden. You needn't retaliate or give weight to any of these rumour mongers.

Christmas on the 25th takes place with the Moon transiting out of your eighth zone of private and sexual matters into the ninth sector of philosophy, religion and higher ideals. What a perfect blend of the worldly with the spiritual. This should be a Christmas full of surprises, revelations and intensely good fortune.

As the year draws to a close, be aware of Mercury, the planet of quick-wittedness, humour and spritely, youthful vivaciousness. Humour will be your catchphrase as 2010 winds down. Use this to decompress any problems in your relationships and to usher in a thoroughly positive 2011.

With Venus continuing its transit through your zone of friendship, my clear forecast for you is that you'll be surrounded by many friends, relatives and genuine admirers. What a great end to an exciting year, Capricorn!

Romance and friendship

When passions are running high, it's easy to feel as if someone is absolutely perfect, which could be the case between the 1st and the 5th. Try to get a grip on yourself and look at things in a clear light. On the 6th, when a friend quietly pats you on the shoulder to point this out, you may not believe them. You should. They are probably seeing a person's character much more clearly than you.

You're not likely to drown in your emotions on the 7th and the 8th, but it's best to keep a lid on how you feel rather than sharing your thoughts too openly with others. This could be tantamount to social suicide! Keep your cards close to your chest.

You can settle old scores before Christmas and, in particular between the 14th and the 19th, speak to others about forgiveness and let go of old, hurtful resentments that are undermining your personal happiness. It's also not a bad idea to extend this openness to issues still hanging around with family members, maybe with your mother or older females in your family. On the 14th, 21st and 23rd, take the time to say sorry if you truly believe you've transgressed against someone in some way.

'Friendship' is the key word in the last few days of the month. Between the 28th and the 31st, you could find yourself in touch with friends whose positive sides of their characters you've previously overlooked. Forget the negativities of the past and try to foster the good in any of your relationships at the close of the year.

Work and money

Between the 1st and the 7th, you'll be disciplined about your work and want to clear the decks so you can thoroughly enjoy Christmas this year. Don't forget that you must balance your physical needs with getting your deadlines met.

You might not want to be with others, even if they're trying to be helpful, between the 6th and the 10th. You need to be diplomatic in hiding from them. It's in this period that some unique solutions are likely to be discovered by you and you'll want to take full credit for that as well.

You'll be relentless in your application of effort to get across the finishing line between the 14th and the 19th. Don't push too hard, however, because there is a tendency to injure or exhaust yourself through long hours and having a workaholic approach to your profession.

The lunar eclipse on the 21st is important in helping you understand your motivations for working and what truly matters in life. If you don't quite complete all your work, relax and enjoy Christmas and remember that you'll have plenty of time in 2011 to tidy up those loose odds and ends.

Destiny dates

Positive: 9, 10, 11, 12, 13, 20, 22, 24, 25, 28, 29, 30, 31

Negative: None

Mixed: 1, 2, 3, 4, 5, 6, 7, 8, 14, 15, 16, 17, 18, 19, 21, 23

2011:
Month by Month Predictions

Time is a companion that goes with us on a journey. It reminds us to cherish each moment, because it will never come again. What we leave behind is not as important as how we have lived.

—Captain Jean-Luc Picard, played by Patrick Stewart
in the film *Star Trek Generations*

Highlights of the month

It's time for a new you, Capricorn, and, with the new Moon occurring in your Sun sign, you can rest assured that this is an important month for you in terms of 'renovating' your personality. Between the 1st and the 3rd you will feel up beat but may find yourself at odds with others in your workplace around the 4th.

The solar eclipse on the same day means that the process of becoming a better person also entails discovering things about yourself that you may not particularly like. This will not be easy, but if you look at yourself in an unbiased manner, you can take some great strides in self-development and come out the other end feeling fantastic about yourself.

People around you are going to see a big change in you this year and, throughout January, you will be proud of some of your accomplishments. You have the drive and energy to achieve a considerable amount. After the 10th you may have a surplus of energy and may even want to help others complete tasks in which they are falling behind.

When the Sun travels through the sign of Capricorn, as it does throughout December and January, you will also feel a much greater sense of popularity and connectedness to the world around you. Your health should also be tiptop. If you've had any longstanding illnesses or discomfort in your body, this is a period when you need to rest so you can overcome those difficulties and feel free of any aches and pains.

Between the 12th and the 16th you'll be much more focused on monetary issues, but be careful not to allow these topics to interfere with your personal relationships. Your lifestyle and desire to spend money on those things you feel are important may be at odds with the perspective of your partner. This requires considerable compromise from both ends of the table, so be prepared to make some allowances. In the end you'll probably find that the criticisms being aimed at you are more than likely correct and you may need to eat some humble pie to adjust yourself to these new realisations.

An important transit after the 23rd highlights the importance of family life and getting down into the nitty-gritty of your personal relationships with relatives. Spend time talking about how you feel and don't shut yourself off from other family members.

As is usual with many born under Capricorn, work usually takes precedence in your life. Family matters can take a backseat when in fact you should be doing more to foster your personal relationships. Use this time, for example, to go out and take leisurely strolls with your loved ones. And, of course, if you're a parent, reconnect with your children to find the inner child within yourself.

Romance and friendship

Between the 1st and the 4th of January, a friend in difficult circumstances may lead you to believe that they're in a worse condition than they are. This will chew up inordinate amounts of your time and have you tied up in emotional knots yourself, because you feel compassion is the way to go. By all means, listen to their problems, but try to sort out any fact from fiction.

Expect a few tense moments after the 5th, but keep in mind that many of your thoughts and concerns are probably self-manufactured. In other words, the situation is not as bad as you think. Jump out of your own mind for a while and simply accept things for the way they are.

For example, you'll need to have a discussion with a close friend who's planning to make romantic moves on you. Explaining your position to them will help calm them down and will give you a sense of control as well as winning their respect.

Between the 8th and the 11th you'll have to write down some new set of guidelines for the way you'd like social contacts to deal with you. Lay low and preserve your peace of mind by showing them the new you.

Mercury has a powerful influence over your communication and, between the 15th and the 22nd, it's likely your mind will feel much more rested once you clear the air and talk about how you feel and what you need in love. The other party may also feel just as relieved to get something off their conscience, as well.

You need to find appropriate outlets for your sexual energy between the 24th and the 30th. Mars and Venus are powerful influences in your emotional life during this period. This could be a double-edged sword and may, on the one hand, be outrageously enjoyable or, on the other hand, be psychologically challenging. An older individual may actually be able to help you find balance through this period.

Work and money

Between the 2nd and the 5th of January you feel a little vulnerable, perhaps due to your inability to grasp some of the technical aspects of the financial and tax issues that are looming. Seek the advice of someone else, and don't be embarrassed about being honest that you are not quite up to par with your knowledge.

Use your mental skills to reconsider alternatives at work. You know, you don't need a licence to think creatively and, even though the Sun—which is in difficult aspect with Saturn around the 8th—may inhibit some of your fast-paced creative thinking, this effect will pass. So, please don't for a minute think that you're stuck where you are forever. Think ahead and, of course, think big!

There's some glory to be achieved at work between the 12th and the 16th. You should bathe in the limelight and enjoy any sort of accolade that comes your way. However, too much humility may be misunderstood, so balance it with an acknowledgement of others' appreciation for a job well done.

On the 18th and 24th you are reactive and need to curb your temper. Put your energy into a self-help program or educational pursuit, especially on the 26th and the 27th.

You are detective-like between the 26th and the 31st. You need to dedicate yourself to understanding the motivations of others. Psychology and other technical topics for expanding your skill set will be of interest and use to you.

Destiny dates

Positive: 17, 18, 19, 20, 21, 22, 23

Negative: 5

Mixed: 1, 2, 3, 4, 8, 9, 10, 11, 12, 13, 14, 15, 16, 24, 25, 26, 27, 28, 29, 30

Highlights of the month

Your interest in financial matters continues into February, spotlighted by the new Moon in your zone of income on the 3rd. Take the time to investigate the way in which you earn money and how you can streamline your dealings and possibly capitalise on opportunities that have been missed in the past.

Because you have so much zest for life just now, you may be burning the candle at both ends, as they say. You may also find yourself a little confused about your ideals after the 4th. Clarify them as well as your objectives early in the year. Make some commitments and also take the time to work on a few new year resolutions. In this manner you can short cut your way to success.

Because Venus moves through your Sun sign this month, your love life should take a turn for the better. You have an excellent rapport with other people, and members of the opposite sex will find you very attractive. However, you mustn't allow yourself to take advantage of others because it will be very easy to coerce someone into doing your bidding. Use your sexual and magnetic powers wisely, or the laws of karma may turn things back on you and create problems down the track.

Your industriousness will pay off in February, with the Sun, Mars and Mercury creating excellent opportunities in your professional life. Your organisational skills will be noted by your employers, and the days of the 7th, 12th and 14th are all excellent for achieving some minor or even major successes. On the 7th, however, be mindful of the fact that you may be pushing yourself and others a little too hard and could run yourself into the ground. Take adequate rest and be gentle on everyone involved in your work projects.

Your relationships could end up 'going south' around the 19th because of the difficult aspect between Venus and Saturn. You might be put out if someone doesn't treat you the way you feel is appropriate. You could be moody, antagonistic and generally hurt by the fact that someone is not as affectionate as you are. You need to be responsible for your own feelings. Don't be so needy.

Your creative and spiritual visions are on the top of your agenda after the 20th and, up until the 22nd, you have the opportunity to extend yourself creatively, perhaps through some fine art, music, or attending some sort of function that stimulates this aspect of your aspirations.

Travel is on the agenda when the Sun transits your third zone of short journeys after the 25th. You'll be busy and involved, with many day-to-day issues that need clarifying and tidying up. Mixing business with pleasure will lighten your load.

Romance and friendship

Play some sports with the ones you love between the 2nd and the 4th of February. You'll be busy with loads of activities, but being physical is a great way to let off some steam.

You're imaginative, ready to love and prepared to do something a little daring after the 5th. You feel confident in your ability to communicate your feelings and to do it in a tasteful fashion.

Between the 7th and the 10th, someone could be playing an ethical trick on you, questioning your values and trying to make you feel bad for holding fast to some of your belief systems. Don't buy into it.

Between the 11th and 15th you will enter new friendships with great confidence and must not be afraid of the changes taking place, even if at first you think that this could cause some loss. I can assure you that Jupiter's principal energies are that of optimism, hope, expansion and spiritual insight. Trust your intuition during this phase and everything will go to your destiny's plan.

Geomagnetic forces can be the source of some problem for you between the 16th and the 24th, so look into the philosophies of Feng Shui to study how you can better create a space that is relaxing and doesn't disturb your physical, mental and spiritual energies.

There are challenging aspects between Jupiter and Pluto after the 26th. These two planets are usually considered powerbrokers in their right angled phase and can bring about a lot of wasted time and false hopes.

This is also punctuated by the entry of Mars into your zone of activity, communications and mental focus. What this means is that you will not only be tired from excessively wasting your own energy, but may need to deal with emotional discussions and negotiations surrounding you as well.

The romantic pace of your life increases between the 27th and the 28th and may leave you feeling exhilarated. Life is there for living, Capricorn!

Work and money

Things run effortlessly at your workplace between the 2nd and the 5th of February. Your employment's likely to take an agreeable turn. Pressures are lifted and replaced with interesting professional interludes.

Between the 6th and the 14th your generosity is enjoyed by everyone, but there's also the menace of overestimating someone or paying too much for something.

You're aggravated by inconveniences, obstacles and distractions, especially by those with whom you work, from the 17th until the 20th. An improved technique to adjust yourself is required.

You are not particularly full of beans between the 21st and the 23rd, but an intense effort is not mandatory just now, either. There's no point overly pushing things.

Your problems will ferment and churn in your head. You'll end up venting your feelings by being domineering and intolerant with another person in your workplace around the 26th. Hold enough of your breath to maintain diplomacy.

You counter quickly to any transgression that may occur on the 27th; however, you won't react to provocation. Stay out of the way of those who like to bait you.

Destiny dates

Positive: 2, 3, 5, 6, 11, 12, 13, 14, 15, 25, 27, 28
Negative: 16, 17, 18, 19, 23, 24, 26
Mixed: 4, 7, 8, 9, 10, 20, 21, 22

MARCH 2011

Highlights of the month

Between the 1st and the 5th, Venus provides you the opportunity to shine in your workplace and to enjoy the tasks you perform. The responsibilities that you are landed with will not bother you so much and will, in fact, give you an excellent chance to prove your worth to your employers and show others just how capable you really are.

When Venus also dominates your financial landscape after the 9th, you'll want to use your hard-earned cash to create something of beauty. The day-to-day practicalities will lose considerable shine, so try to find ways to enjoy the money you earn in an aesthetic way. Purchasing objects of art or antique furniture, or simply just cleaning out your desk or living space will be the perfect cure for any sort of mental blues you may be feeling.

The cycle of Mercury after the 11th emphasises the fact that you are gaining a greater understanding of your feelings and family relationships. There will be some interest in ferreting out issues from your past, looking through old and nostalgic photographs, and gaining insight into your roots. This curiosity may bring you in touch with people you haven't dealt with for a long time. Expect a mixture of good and bad feelings as you try to figure out your true purpose in life. There may also be some issues relating to real estate.

There is a challenging planetary aspect after the 24th, and this could even involve a head-on confrontation with an employer over the way you are performing your tasks. It could be difficult because standing up to an authority figure could jeopardise your position, but under these transits you will hold your ground and probably have good moral reasons for doing so. If you don't win the argument you will gain the respect of someone more powerful than you.

There is a period of awkwardness between the 20th and the 25th. Mercury makes it difficult for you to think clearly and expressing your ideas the way you want to may prove to be more difficult than you first thought. It's at times like these that you need to jot down your ideas to see what's on your mind rather than fumbling your way through a meeting or a discussion. This will have more relevance if you are a keynote speaker or someone having to share ideas with a group.

After the 30th you will take up an added interest in writing, poetry or other forms of literary expression and will generally feel more connected to people. If up to now you haven't spent much time with a sibling, this is the moment to reconnect because your interests may turn out to be in sync with them. You may also read something that has a large impact on your life.

Romance and friendship

You'll know straightaway whether or not you should be spending more time with a person, or giving them the flick. Between the 1st and 7th of March you will also apply these psychic responses to many circumstances in your life. Begin practising these abilities within you as much as possible.

Relationships of all types are activated between the 10th and the 13th. Collaboration, conciliation and adjustments to others' viewpoints require your concentration. Focusing on family matters is also highlighted in this period.

You may be using food and other sensual delights to sweep emotional issues under the rug between the 14th and the 18th. Why not simply face up to what's happening to you? You may need to analyse how some facets of your early life have impacted upon your current relationships. Perhaps the food is simply an external manifestation of those emotions you haven't yet looked into or dealt with adequately.

Pay attention to your dreams and seemingly absentminded thoughts between the 19th and the 21st. You could gain some interesting knowledge from them, especially if they relate to premonitions about how to deal with some of your most personal relationships.

Think twice before overreacting or trying to force your intentions on others, regardless of the appropriateness of your actions, between the 22nd and the 25th. Someone you are trying to help may not be as thick-skinned as you imagine.

There may be some boundaries you'll need to set with someone to protect your own best interests and those of others you love. Between the 26th and the 31st, you may realise just how much protection has been involved. Perhaps it was too much.

Work and money

Break free of any old viewpoints that no longer work for you. Just because you believed something yesterday, doesn't mean it's the same today. Between the 1st and the 5th of March, you will be prepared to implement some new and progressive elements in your work routine.

You will somehow need to adjust your way of communicating in order to reach an accord between the 10th and the 13th. It's important to be clear on what you want.

Between 15th and the 19th you may reach an impasse that has come about by being lazy in your job. Picking up the ball and running with it is what is needed. As an alternative to making your ego feel guilty, may I suggest that challenging yourself is a better route out of this situation because it will motivate your energies?

Because you are impatient between the 21st and the 28th, you may do or say things in a hurry that you may later regret. Slow yourself down a touch. You're moving too quickly for those around you.

Your feelings are dynamic yet controlled on the 29th. This is a winning combination for satisfactorily getting things done and keeping your opinion credible.

Destiny dates

Positive: 1, 2, 3, 4, 5, 6, 7, 9, 10, 11, 12, 13

Negative: 22, 23, 24, 25, 26, 27, 28, 31

Mixed: 14, 15, 16, 17, 18, 19, 20, 21, 29, 30

Highlights of the month

Family issues take precedence and may not be all that easy to deal with between the 1st and the 7th. Mars creates turmoil for you, probably because you are overreacting to something that has previously been said or done. Decompress the situation by not making too many bold moves that could jeopardise all the good ground you have gained in your relationships. This is a period when you need to think before you act because later you may regret your actions. Remember, once a word leaves your mouth, you can't take back.

You won't particularly need anyone when Venus and the Sun shower you with their blessings between the 10th and the 15th. It is possible for you to feel comfortable in your own skin and appreciate your own personality without needing others to stroke your ego. You may receive some sort of accolade or at least a compliment about the way you have been conducting yourself, and this could come from someone older than yourself who appreciates who you are. This will instil confidence in you and make you feel quite happy.

You have considerably more charm this month, with Venus giving you the opportunity to apply for a job, go on a new date or arrange appointments in which you have a greater impact on those you deal with. Take full advantage of these energies, because this is a lucky period. What you say and do will be received very well by others. Expect some success, based upon your charming and persuasive qualities.

You may make a purchase this month. It could be a big-ticket item such as a car, boat or something else expensive that has been on your mind for some time. Between the 24th and the 27th, feel free to pat yourself on the back or show your self-appreciation by buying yourself a gift. It's about time you realise that you do deserve to give yourself something of value from time to time.

You are accident prone after the 25th. Tread carefully and make sure you have planned your schedule well. Allow adequate time to arrive at your destination safely without rushing and speeding, especially if you are driving. Don't engage people in arguments, even if you believe you are correct.

When the Sun enters your fifth zone of creativity, you will sense that a new cycle of experiences has commenced and is starting to peak around the 29th. If you are a parent this is a particularly wonderful phase where you take the time to listen to your children's needs and also to play with them. You will feel youthful again.

Romance and friendship

You're in the mood to spend extra time within your family circle, in the comfort of your own home, between the 1st and the 5th of April. Take this time to consider all that you have to be grateful for and all you can give. You're inspired to take tranquil action with family members or relatives. Use this period to help mediate on any disputes that have been festering for some time. Also, set aside an hour or two of personal time for a bath or a relaxing reading session.

A friend or loved one may require much of your time on the 7th, but you may be otherwise distracted in a world of your own, failing to spot the vital signals. Be a little more alert to your friends' needs.

Emotional disagreements are possible between the 10th and 14th, so you'll need to be as aware as possible of the state of affairs of another person's feelings.

On the 16th, buy yourself that memento or trinket you've been dreaming about. Attach to it some past memories of a wonderful day and carry it with you to remind you of positive things.

You could be duped into getting mixed up in a passionate affair between the 17th and the 19th. As alluring as it is to pretend you're playing the lead role in a major motion picture, you must resolve to extricate yourself from such emotional melodramas.

Be aware of the generosity of another's love between the 21st and the 24th. Don't underestimate an important gesture. Be especially sure to notice it if it is from someone younger than you.

You could be impatient between the 25th and the 27th because those around you appear to be dragging their feet while you want to fly. This may be a case of having to fly solo.

Communication along private lines, such as corresponding with a comrade or telephoning a family member, is favoured between the 28th and the 30th. Reach out to them and reconnect.

Work and money

Anticipate last-minute changes and adjustments to your timetable after the 3rd of April. Have a backup to your plan just in case it all goes awry. Badly chosen timing or annoying hitches concerning papers, contracts and meetings will lead to rewording or redoing an application or proposal.

You see the need to set the agenda between the 5th and the 10th so that others don't later take over the controls! Get in there and get a grip of any potentially overpowering situations.

You can discuss important matters with strong support from co-workers between the 13th and the 20th. Don't hold back, but word things delicately to avoid miscommunication.

Have fun between the 22nd and the 25th, but try not to let reckless spending leave you saddled with bills afterwards. In this case, the bills will over-shadow the goods. Half of being smart is knowing what you're dumb at. If you can figure out your shortcomings, you can work harder at making them attributes!

Enter demolition phase! So, something has gone wrong. But is it past the point of fixing? It's best to break everything down and start completely afresh on the 27th.

Destiny dates

Positive: 15, 16, 28, 29, 30

Negative: None

Mixed: 1, 2, 3, 4, 5, 6, 7, 8, 9, 10, 11, 12, 13, 14, 17, 18, 19, 20, 21, 22, 23, 24, 25, 26, 27

Highlights of the month

It's one of those months where relationships could be so challenging that you seriously contemplate getting out of them completely. Between the 1st and the 6th, Venus, Mars and Mercury conspire to cause you doubts, make you feel at a loss emotionally and overall give you a sense that love is not really worth pursuing at all. You know in your heart of hearts that this is not really the case and that life comes in cycles, which is what the movement of the planets reflects.

Fortunately, after the 10th, the Sun and also Mercury and Venus bring you a completely new set of positive energies that you can utilise to overcome these relationship obstacles. Sweet talk, emotional and intellectual compassion and synchronicity will be very likely after this date. Then, when Mars enters your fifth zone of love and romance on the 11th, you will be fired up once again with great confidence to make your relationships and your closest friend-ships work all that much better.

Don't be afraid to mix with people who have very different views and live a lifestyle that may seem somewhat strange to you. Here is your opportunity to broaden your outlook and understand topics in which you may not previously have been interested. From the 15th until the 20th, explore different avenues of communication, philosophy and religion. You could find yourself in the company of some rather unusual and very interesting people.

There is a hint by Mercury that after the 22nd you might take a more speculative approach to your finances; and this is quite okay, as long as you have the appropriate information and advice, as well as the support to do so in an intelligent and cautious manner.

The stock market may be the perfect arena for you to try your hand at making money and invest-ing some of your hard-earned cash. With Venus also entering this same area of your horoscope around the 23rd, this could turn out to be a collaborative venture with a friend or a partner.

You have a strong sporting urge, given the influence of Mars on you after the 26th. You want to get physical, lose weight and move your body in an outdoor environment. As well as bringing you a higher level of physical vitality, this will also work towards giving you mental clarity and emotional stability. It's not a bad idea to get those endorphins circulating throughout your system this month.

The Sun brings you excellent opportunities to do with job-related activities between the 27th and the 30th. Some of your practical insights will be the reason that you are singled out to take on a leadership role or speak on behalf of your company or organisation.

Romance and friendship

Your mind tends towards your family; in particular, your mother, on the 1st and 2nd of May. There are lessons to be considered from the past that impact personal areas of your life at this time.

You want to give to your friends and loved ones and may generously spend some time or money in an effort to make them happy between the 4th and 7th. Just don't make them feel embarrassed by spending too much.

You slip out of work mode into a more relaxed style of living between the 10th and the 14th. This will make life a little easier than expected and you will certainly want to push all demands to one side.

Your mind and heart are at odds with each other between the 16th and the 18th, fighting it out for supremacy in your being at the moment. Listen to both, then be decisive in your action.

You may have to grin and bear a social situation between the 20th and the 22nd, in which the guests or visitors are anything but entertaining. Don't worry, it will pass. Just learn to be a better actor. Indeed, this is, in all reality, a time to weigh up your appearance and your associations and begin to make some significant changes for the better.

You need to be in somebody's company and share devoted feelings with them between the 23rd and the 25th. You're physically drained and need emotional replenishment. You are also ripe for a flight of fancy, so delay any major decisions of an emotional nature.

Your emotions are close to the surface right now, so you are likely to react spontaneously to any kind of stimulus between the 26th and the 30th. It's a first-rate time to take action but this may turn out to be behaviour that is really out of your usual character. Enjoy it, nonetheless.

Hang on: don't put your foot in it on the 31st! Try your best to think about what it is you are trying to communicate when it comes to a certain older person on that day.

Work and money

Always—I repeat, always—prepare a promissory note when you loan money to friends, or vice versa. You need to be clear on what's involved between the 3rd and the 6th of May. How much has been loaned and the terms of repayment are essential records.

If you've overlooked some of these precautionary measures in the past, it's quite possible that some past debt or loan may rear its head and you may be ill-equipped through poor self-management in dealing with this issue.

However, the rewards you've been working so hard for and looking forward to, may emerge unnoticed between the 11th and the 16th. It won't be that long till you see some truly positive and remarkable results.

You wish for a break from your usual schedule and, because you're willing to experiment, you can experience a refreshing change of pace, especially after the 17th.

A new talent or flair in some aspect of your work will emerge between the 18th and the 22nd. Even if you're not able to capitalise on this, it will give you a sense of creative purpose.

Adopting alternative measures is a must between the 25th and the 31st. Sticking to the usual formal procedures just isn't going to cut it with your lower level of patience.

Destiny dates

Positive: 10, 11, 12, 13, 14, 15, 19, 31

Negative: 24

Mixed: 1, 2, 4, 5, 6, 7, 16, 17, 18, 20, 21, 22, 23, 25, 26, 27, 28, 29, 30

Highlights of the month

Get ready for some big changes throughout June as Uranus makes its impact felt on your domestic sphere and immediate family affairs. Between the 1st and the 10th, changes are definitely afoot, and you will need to adapt yourself quickly to some of these events, which may hit you without any notice whatsoever.

Usually we like to think that we are the ones in control of our own destiny. But it is times like these that the planets remind us, in no uncertain terms, of just how little control we do have, in fact. Make sure you have Plan B ready to handle any unforeseen occurrences.

As if these changes in your home and domestic lives aren't enough, Uranus also makes its imprint felt on your professional affairs. If you have been kept down, feeling that you are not respected for your ideas and working in a dead-end job for way too long, you will definitely feel the pull of independence.

You will want to spread your wings and fly, and this desire could create some problems if those closest to you are trying to clip those wings of yours. It is a matter of being true to yourself and allowing your spirit to soar.

You could feel overworked between the 12th and the 15th. Increase the dose of your vitamins on a daily basis and don't eat while you're rushing or emotionally stressed out. Your mind and your nervous system could be feeling the impact of the pressure of work and other demands.

After the 16th things move much more smoothly for you and you could find yourself enjoying some kind of social activity within the framework of your professional or business life. This may be a prime opportunity you have been waiting for, to make some important connections that can further your career ambitions. Try connecting with people 'in the know' who will be able to provide you with funding, information or the keys to new and vital networks.

Having too many irons in the fire between the 18th and the 25th is not a good idea. You will find getting anything done very hard indeed if you have taken on too many projects. Your thinking could be muddled and your decision-making processes could falter. Make sure you have someone whom you can bounce your ideas off before giving a commitment that involves money or even time.

Your personal relationships are emphasised after the 26th, and this is a good note with which to end the month. Try to be fair and reasonable in your dealings with your lover or partner, and accentuate the positive aspects of your relationship when communicating to them.

Romance and friendship

The new Moon on the 1st of June in your zone of health warns that you must take care of your physical wellbeing. Don't allow emotional episodes to undermine your physical vitality between the 1st and the 5th. Besides, you have better things on which to spend your energy.

Just when you think you've finally hit the bottom, someone will toss you a shovel. Between the 6th and the 10th, you will be offered a hand. It may not be the hand you want, but show your gratitude because this offer will help lift your spirits again.

Recollections, thoughts of the past or even fragments of dreams come into your mind between the 12th and 14th. These experiences may make you open to new ideas as well as feel less selfish and more compassionate. Therefore, this is a spiritual cycle for you, too.

During the full Moon phase you take some much-needed time out, especially between the 15th and the 17th. Recharge your emotional batteries and take stock of what you want in your love life.

You sense that you aren't as gorgeous as you'd like to be between the 18th and the 22nd. May I suggest you start to work on the inside: eat right, stretch and exercise? You'll be surprised how much better this will make you feel.

You need to be open to the subtle hints of others and liberate the brilliance of your spirit between 23rd and the 26th. If others have a problem, it's theirs to deal with. For your part, you need to air your thoughts and bring to a standstill any suspicions you may have about a friend. Make sure you know what the specific issues surrounding them are first.

You may be asked to be present at a pleasant event or take a trip between the 27th and the 30th. Don't hold back just because it's not planned. Incidentally, be clear about the difference between love and lust at this time.

Work and money

Allow others the space to believe what they want, and hopefully they will respect your viewpoints, too. Mars is shaking things up for you, particularly around the 5th of June, when it influences the Sun in your ninth zone of creativity. Be careful in your sporting activities, as well, during the phase of the 6th until the 8th.

Between the 10th and the 15th you may be rushing to meet deadlines, speeding to your destination and not really paying attention to the moment. This is when mishaps can happen, and the last thing you want is to find yourself tripping up. Take things a little more slowly and become more aware of what you're doing.

Try to look where you can become most efficient in your work, especially between the 18th and the 20th. Eliminate those activities that are consuming much of your time with little or no result. Using this technique will help you maximise your resources.

Thoughts of relocating are also on the cards. Contractual Mercury causes you to seek out real estate deals after the 21st and up until the 30th. Talk to your accountant or other financial adviser before committing yourself to any long-term debt.

Destiny dates

Positive: 16, 17, 26, 28, 29, 30

Negative: 11

Mixed: 1, 2, 3, 4, 5, 6, 7, 8, 9, 10, 12, 13, 14, 15, 18, 19, 20, 21, 22, 23, 24, 25

Highlights of the month

The favourable aspect of Mars to Saturn in your career zone is excellent for constructive work that will give you a sense of purpose and achievement. What you do between the 1st and the 6th may not be altogether creatively fulfilling, but you can't always live life as if it is a bed of roses. This is the cycle where your focus and tenacity to complete projects gives you an insight you may not have had before. You're toughening up and are now able to see the bigger picture.

By not discarding all the traditions, instead blending them with some of the more progressive technologies available, you will put yourself in a better position to achieve long-term success. This is not the time to dismiss those who have a wealth of experience, for the sake of keeping up with modern fads. Try to find some equilibrium between the two extremes.

On the 9th the planets Venus and Pluto enter into a rather complex tangle, which could mean you are not able to resolve some aspect of love. After the 10th you have to do some investigative work and this will predominantly relate to finance, money, facts and figures. It could, however, also have something to do with a deeper understanding of a relationship.

This may concern issues of jealousy, posses- siveness and other negative emotions that impact poorly on your long-term prospects for a happy rela- tionship. Try to get above these erosive, emotional states.

You may or may not act upon the impulse to throw all cares to the wind, but when Mars affects your career domain around the 13th, you will begin to be much more practical than usual, feeling the responsibility of your commitments. Mars makes you impulsive but fortunately your Capricorn nature puts the brakes on behaviour that is short-sighted in any way.

Such things as your health, your work and your daily routine will take on a new significance and you could be rather preoccupied with these matters. You could come crashing back down to earth, trying to reorganise your life in a way that is befitting of the commitments you've made in the past. You will try to find a more adequate balance between what you desire and what others are expecting of you.

Marriage and/or business contracts steal the show after the 15th. If you're not yet 'hitched', you could be one of the lucky Capricorn-born individ- uals who can now look forward to an engagement or marriage and, if this doesn't happen to be your own, it could be that of a friend or close family member. In any case, some sort of celebration is likely to take place.

Between the 27th and the 31st the opportunity to enter into some sort of workplace relationship is indicated. If this is not a full-blown love affair, you may still feel some strong heart connection with someone at your workplace.

Romance and friendship

From the 1st to the 4th of July you mustn't allow responsibility to get the better of you. The Sun and Saturn create a heaviness around you that makes you much more serious than you need to be.

You are idealistic about your love affairs between the 5th and the 7th, but you may also be talking a little too much about your feelings to people who may use these words against you. Be careful with whom you share your trusted secrets. Not everyone is your best friend.

You are able to sort out some serious issues with your lover or partner from the 8th till the 11th. Your use of power will be inspirational and will lift the person's spirits and also empower them. Their respect will come your way due to a conversation you have together.

Your self-esteem is at a peak between the 12th and the 14th, when your energy causes you to be the centre of attention, the life of the party. But you are also prone to overdoing it. You may be aloof towards one person in particular with whom you normally spend most of your time. Don't let an ostentatious mood ruin the party.

On the spur of the moment you may decide to take on some social leadership role that is beyond your capability. The period of the 15th to the 18th requires you to be a little more humble and accept that you are not an expert in every department. Ask for the help of a friend if you choose to continue with this course of action.

Your sexual affairs occupy a great deal of your attention from the 23rd to the 28th. You want excitement, intimacy and a change of pace, which your lover will give you. Romance is in the air!

A short journey with a friend on the 30th may be surrounded by an air of mystery or confusion. Clarify the details before you purchase your tickets.

Work and money

Expectations of your performance are so high that you may decide to throw in the towel between the 2nd and the 6th of July. You mustn't let others dictate the terms of your work or deadlines. Don't under-estimate the power you have in your role. You do in fact have the respect of your colleagues and your performance is better than you think.

New contacts appearing through your work offer exciting, fresh opportunities to further your career, especially between the 7th and the 12th. Key dates that affect you positively include the 7th, 9th and 10th.

An argument is looming with your employer around the 11th, so be prepared with your facts and figures rather than scrambling to improvise on the spot. You will not achieve a good outcome by pretending you know the answer.

Your intuitive powers can serve you well between the 12th and 20th. If you have a gut feeling about a course of action on a deal, follow it.

Financial matters need careful attention between the 25th and the 30th. This task may not be fun but, if you give your full attention to the task at hand, you'll clear your desk of a lot of tedious paperwork and feel refreshed.

Destiny dates

Positive: 8, 10, 12, 14, 19, 20, 23, 24, 25, 26, 27, 28, 29, 31

Negative: None

Mixed: 1, 2, 3, 4, 5, 6, 7, 9, 11, 13, 15, 16, 17, 18, 30

Highlights of the month

As August kicks off you find yourself in a more unusual state of mind, taking an interest in psychological topics and the mysteries and philosophies of life and death. Of course, sex and the secret aspects of intimacy are also part and parcel of the Sun's transit through your eighth zone of mystery.

From the 1st till the 4th these perspectives may demand more attention from you; you will want some clear answers to the questions that arise from within. This is a great phase because it pushes you further and further into yourself to seek answers about life; not from others, not from books or self-styled gurus, but from within your deepest, spiritual nature.

Your attention this month could also be grabbed by some lingering issue relating to taxation or shared resources within your family. Resolve these problems, particularly between the 5th and the 10th. If you have been lavish in your spending and not putting aside enough money for your tax bill, this could be a big lesson for you.

Your financial obligations will be bothersome but, if you examine your past history as to how you arrived at this place in your life, it will be clear that you may not have been disciplined enough and this is the lesson of the transits occurring in your horoscope this month.

You have a strongly generous disposition between the 11th and 15th, so you'll find yourself thinking about how to show your appreciation to a friend who has stood by you over the long haul. By the same token, you will be surprised by a gift that is also offered to you. Some of your friends could also be feeling appreciative of your commitment to their relationship with you. This is certainly a time of mutual affection and for deepening the bonds of friendship.

You want to understand culture and foreign affairs more readily during the period of the 18th to the 25th. Educational pursuits may also take a front seat, when you consider what topics or subjects you wish to explore to indulge your mind. You might enrol in a correspondence course to expand your mental horizons.

Between the 28th and the 30th you will find yourself dealing with relationships of an intense and personal nature. Transforming yourself and your partner will be your key concern. However, remember to focus predominantly on your own issues because forcing your views on another may backfire.

Romance and friendship

You have some good karma in your relationships throughout August, and affairs of the heart will suddenly escalate for the better between the 1st and the 5th. However, be careful to not give too strong a commitment around the 3rd, when Mercury goes retrograde.

Mars conjoins your zone of marriage after the 3rd, too, so be wary of contentious issues and pushing your opinions too strongly. Your partner may retaliate if you try to get them to adopt your lines of thinking. Get their side of the story as well.

Mercury is in good aspect to Mars between the 4th and the 7th, so talk about important issues at this time because you will be forceful and persuasive in a diplomatic fashion that yields good results.

From the 9th to the 12th, don't be afraid to let others see your best side. Being humble is not in your best interest now, even if you truly believe that big-noting yourself will leave others with a bad opinion of you. Indeed, it serves you well in a social situation to step out into the limelight and attract the best attention you possibly can.

From the 13th till the 15th the circle of friends in which you find yourself may cause you to be more serious than you need to be. Lighten up and enjoy the situation, even if you feel like a fish out of water.

From the 16th until the 23rd don't hold out for an apology that you may never get. Learn to forgive people or shift them out of your life. Move on to better times.

A simple change of heart isn't going to be enough to fix an issue between the 24th and the 28th. You'll need to be accommodating of the other person's viewpoint.

Playing the field on the 30th will be fun but may also not give you exactly what you're looking for.

Work and money

Activities surrounding your finances may reach a feverish pitch by the 13th of August, when the full Moon occurs in your zone of income. Up until then, the 2nd, 3rd, 5th and 8th are dates when you need to pay more attention to the ins and outs of monetary matters. Reduce waste, curb your spending appetite and live more frugally until you get on top of your finances.

A consultative approach is necessary between the 10th and the 12th if you're planning some sort of social or business get-together on the home front. Otherwise you may astonish family members when guests roll up without their knowledge. Surprises are not the way to go.

From the 13th until the 19th, your moneymaking schemes make a lot of sense. If you need money, support or some sort of direction generally, approach those with experience with an air of congeniality and mutual assistance. Use all the resources available to you.

Around the 23rd try not to let your impulses cause you to make rash decisions. A good idea doesn't necessarily have to be acted upon immediately.

From the 24th till the 30th procedures go well and business negotiations are hassle free.

Destiny dates

Positive: 1, 2, 4, 11, 12

Negative: 8

Mixed: 3, 5, 6, 7, 9, 10, 13, 14, 15, 16, 17, 18, 19, 20, 21, 22, 23, 24, 25, 26, 27, 28, 29, 30

SEPTEMBER 2011

Highlights of the month

Some of your hard work finally pays off in September. With Venus making a return journey to a positive part of your horoscope, you can rest assured that its influence will catapult you into the good books with people who can make a difference to your future.

Once again, it's time to tidy up your resumé and make those phone calls to recruitment agencies and other influential individuals who can help you in your search for the perfect job. Between the 2nd and the 6th, you should make an extra effort to put your best foot forward. Don't be afraid to advertise yourself and become better known for your skills and past achievements.

Your past could be playing on your mind between the 11th and the 17th. You can only move forward if you release yourself from past issues in relationships that have held you back. Bottling up your emotions and sweeping them under the rug will only continue to make you feel uneasy about the way a friendship or relationship has finished. Why not do what you know needs to be done and call the person in question to sort out any remaining differences?

The transit of Venus in the upper part of your horoscope must surely be one of the highlights of the year for you. You can move ahead professionally with such ease that you're probably wondering why this is the case. Thank lucky Venus! Not a great deal of effort needs to be made for you to enjoy not only your work, but also the people and the additional benefits that go with it. Between the 19th and 23rd you will be enjoying what you're doing, sharing the benefits and looking forward to even greater success.

Saturn has provided you with tremendous focus and discipline this year, but after the 25th, it may cause you to feel somewhat cramped in your rela-tionships. Given that you've felt so good about your work and yourself, it could come as a surprise that your self-worth, and the image you have of yourself, may not be up to par.

As much as you try to convey your feelings, you may feel stifled in your style of communication. You probably have so much on your plate that rushing may be what is creating the confusion. Cutting back on some of your workload will be essential to give you the space you need to re-establish your true self.

Mercury and the Sun put you in a position to resolve many of these stifling mental states up to the 28th. You will reorient yourself and start to get back on track to implement some of your ambitious schemes. You'll be practical and will do whatever it takes to achieve your goals.

Romance and friendship

Your passionate approaches to loved ones may meet resistance between the 1st and the 5th of September. Even if you are generous with your feelings on the 3rd, a lover may not understand your intention or could inadvertently assume that you have some ulterior motive.

On the 6th you are amorous but must not play games with someone's emotions or heart. By the 8th you will leave them dazed and confused. Be straight with your feelings.

The full Moon on the 12th takes place in your zone of communications. As well as talking a lot and reaching some important conclusions in your love life, you may also choose to travel quite a bit. Travelling with others, communicating with those at a distance, hustling and bustling with loads of social activities, makes you a butterfly at this time. Keep your wits about you, however, because moments of inattentiveness could cause you to forget or lose things.

Don't be too aggressive about how you wish to be treated between the 13th and the 19th. This period indicates urgent demands and also subtle forces at play. Emotional blackmail is likely.

An exciting new phase begins for you from the 20th to the 25th. A clever approach to dealing with a relative or neighbour is justification for patting yourself on the back. You manage to sidestep an argument.

You are feisty, irritable and also impatient for a change between the 26th and the 29th. Others can't understand you or find it difficult to keep up with your pace.

On the 30th you'll be able to step back in sync with your peer group but you will still feel some frustration at the fact that they are dragging their feet.

Work and money

You are buzzing with new ideas for moneymaking during the period of the 1st until the 8th of September. Some of these concepts may be way over the heads of those you are trying to impress, so try to speak using plain language, otherwise they could miss your point.

Between the 9th and 15th you start to work on some legal or bureaucratic issues. The new Moon this month, on the 27th, occurs in your legal zone, so make sure you prepare well. Those of you who are having ongoing legal battles have a breakthrough occurring around the 16th.

Between the 17th and the 19th you don't feel as though you have the support of those upon whom you have previously relied. Independence is your key word for the time being.

The Sun transits your zone of career and reputation after the 23rd, indicating an excellent period for you throughout the remainder of the month. A new work project, albeit temporary, may bolster your self-confidence and open a new door to a more permanent and lucrative position in future.

On the 29th and 30th, your constructive writing skills will have a favourable result on some negotiation. Helping others to write more clearly will be appreciated.

Destiny dates

Positive: 9, 10, 20, 21, 22, 23, 24, 30

Negative: 8, 13, 18

Mixed: 1, 2, 3, 4, 5, 6, 11, 12, 13, 14, 15, 16, 17, 19, 25, 26, 27, 28, 29

Highlights of the month

You must again tend with some serious responsibilities from the 1st until the 5th. You will realise that you can't use your charm to get you through some of the meetings and confrontational episodes that occur. Saturn, Mars and Venus don't in any way give you relief and you could be working hard with very little recognition.

For those of you who are home-makers, this point could be driven home by the fact that you feel unsupported and will be left doing most of the chores without any real appreciation. You will have to put your foot down, that's for sure!

Control issues over money will be foremost in your mind between the 6th and 10th. Although your earning capacity is enhanced, you're probably wondering why you are not getting ahead. Could it be that someone else is 'riding your back'—a partner, child, needy relative or friend—who just don't seem to be managing their own money well enough and expects you to foot the bill? You may also start to feel obligated in social situations where people conveniently don't have enough cash to pay the costs and you will be left picking up the tab. You will get to the point where enough is enough!

Throughout this month, especially after the 11th and up until the 15th, you may well start to lose a sense of who you are. Those wonderfully warm feelings and strong sense of self-esteem will evaporate—but fortunately, only temporarily. Being used by others will make you feel like a doormat. However, it is around the 16th, when Venus enters a better phase socially for you, that you are able to smooth over the difficulties and regain your sense of self-respect.

You will also coincidentally find yourself in the company of one or two other people who are going through exactly the same sort of phase. These issues of non-appreciation may be better handled by sharing your experiences with those of like-mind. This will be a constructive period in which you will draw some important conclusions about how you can act to make some radical changes, especially on the home front.

The exciting and young mind of Mercury enters your social sphere around this time and between the 18th and the 22nd there could be a load of social occasions in which you could find yourself letting your hair down and thoroughly enjoying yourself.

There could be an association with a much younger person who teaches you the art of expanding your mind and not limiting yourself to what you believe is necessarily 'your thing'. This is a great period and one in which humour and entertainment will be very much highlighted, particularly from the 25th till the 30th.

Romance and friendship

Up until the 4th of October, control issues will dominate your relationships. Your sex life and deep, unresolved feelings and transformational processes are part of the game of love for you right now. Challenges centre on having to prove yourself to be better than the next person. You're probably outgrowing many standard modes of relating to others and this will challenge your partner.

Between the 5th and the 8th you may experience difficulty conveying your ideas, so be careful not to say the wrong thing. Be clear-headed because some of your ideas will be misconstrued. You're highly strung as a result of an abundance of nervous energy. It could be that you need to get out and do additional physical exercise to balance your drives.

Between the 9th and the 12th your personality will come across as too strong for some of your friends and new acquaintances. However, this time it is not you who has to change, because it is those around you who are weak.

Between the 11th and the 15th, someone will be testing your limits. You must understand your own boundaries if you are to deal appropriately with the issues being presented to you.

Group activities take on a new meaning between the 16th and the 20th. Friends will play a vital role in your life, but this could also be a time when some of them may have to be removed from your life as well. You need to sift the wheat from the chaff, as they say.

You will make concessions to someone in authority who likes to control things. Between the 22nd and the 25th you will be severely tested but will come out the other end feeling as if you have become a better person. Discipline and controlled speech will be difficult but fulfilling.

Between the 26th and the 31st you will be inspired to take up a new activity that involves colour, design, harmony and balance. Artistic works, interior design and other types of craft will attract you.

Work and money

You can either work hard or work smart between the 1st and 12th of October. Just because you spend more hours on a particular task doesn't mean that it is going to turn out any better. A clever way to work just now is to find shortcuts to achieve the same results.

Between the 13th and the 18th you have to convince someone of the benefits they will receive by using your proposed method. You may have some competition at this time, but clear, concise expression will see you victorious over your opponents.

Your ability for creative vision between the 19th and the 23rd is shown by the presence of Venus and Neptune and spills over into your financial activities. You'll see the 'art' involved in business. Those Capricorns who have not yet developed a taste for money can regard this as a time when such an understanding will happen.

Keep asking questions if you are not getting the answers you want. From the 24th to the 28th, you hit on the right formula for gaining access to information that was previously out of reach. You will discover secrets that you should not have. Confidentiality is critical in your business relationships.

Destiny dates

Positive: 16, 17, 18, 19, 20, 21, 26, 27, 28, 29, 30

Negative: None

Mixed: 1, 2, 3, 4, 5, 6, 7, 8, 9, 10, 11, 12, 13, 14, 15, 22, 23, 24, 25

Highlights of the month

A new Moon is usually a signal of something commencing for you, a new cycle after the closing off of a previous cycle. Between the 1st and the 10th the opportunity for a fresh romance is quite likely for those born under Capricorn. But this may not fully manifest until later in the month, on the 25th, when the new Moon affects your love affairs. The earlier full Moon on the 10th brings your feelings to fruition and it could be at this time that you see a romantic opportunity on the horizon.

You must be careful that your feelings don't get the better of you, especially between the 11th and the 14th. There are some unusual twists and turns in your love life as Venus enters the quiet and somewhat secretive area of the horoscope.

You may want a clandestine liaison. You could be longing for something or someone that has not been available to you in your current circumstances, and this may heighten your curiosity to a larger extent than usual. You will not want to listen to the good advice of friends, who are also warning you of the same thing that I am, which is, 'don't play with fire'.

The mountain of energy you currently possess could erupt, so to speak, if you don't pace yourself. Burnout is quite likely between the 19th and 23rd. The limits of your patience may also be tested during this same period, when others push your 'hot' buttons. Patience will be absolutely essential if you are to manage this planetary cycle in the best possible way.

When Mercury goes retrograde on the 24th, some of your plans may have to be put on hold. However, you mustn't get angry about this change in circumstance because it may not necessarily mean failure but simply a reassessment of what you are hoping to achieve, and when. You must watch the impact of Saturn on your Sun sign around the 26th because you could feel rather depressed that these plans haven't yet gone the way you expected.

On the 27th and the 28th you can feel completely comfortable in accepting an invitation to go somewhere or do something that is extraordinary. There may be an element of fantasy attached to the outing; for example, a masquerade party, a trip to some sort of avant-garde hotel or event, or simply a concert that is rather unique in its presentation, like Cirque du Soleil.

Around the 30th an unexpected change in the status of an employer or co-worker could create an element of doubt or fear in you and others with whom you work. Maintain your poise and don't let the unknown rattle you.

Romance and friendship

The severity of an itch is inversely proportional to your ability to reach it. If someone is annoying you, what can you do about it? Perhaps not a great deal straightaway. So, be patient and careful between the 1st and the 5th of November. This period could relate to a seven-year itch, making it quite powerful.

Curb your appetite for things you cannot have between the 6th and the 8th. It's only a matter of time until you will have what you most desire. Redirect these energies into a creative outlet.

Actions speak louder than words between the 11th and the 13th. Let people know exactly how much you appreciate them by giving them a positive reception.

One of the laws of power states that it's better to exhibit disregard for the things you can't have rather than beg for them. This means you don't have to be needy in order to get your lover, or the person you are interested in, to show some affection towards you. Between the 14th and the 18th, use this strategy during a romantic interlude.

Don't be gullible between the 19th and the 24th. Just because someone has said they are on your side doesn't mean they haven't said the same thing to others as well. There could be an element of deception in your friendships during this phase.

The new Moon on the 25th takes place in your zone of friendships. You could meet someone who transforms your view of the world and gives you a great deal to think about. This will stimulate your mind and give you a renewed sense of purpose. However, some of the things they are saying to you could be hard to implement after the 27th. You don't need to do everything today. Pace yourself.

Work and money

If, between the 1st and 10th of November, you don't feel a deep, passionate love for your work, it may be that you have momentarily ventured down the wrong street of life. Reassess your options before spending any more time and money on your current course.

Between the 11th and the 14th, it's your time to shine. People may try to cut you down but it is up to you to ignore this petty behaviour and reach for the stars.

If co-workers and friends are draining your wallet and proving to be a financial burden, remember the old Chinese proverb: 'Give a man a fish and he will eat for a day. Teach a man to fish and he will eat for the rest of his life.' Employ this wisdom between the 15th and 18th.

There's no point arguing about something you may know a lot about but can't convince others that you do. Understand that the truth will come to light between the 19th and 24th.

You'll feel envious about a friend and their progress professionally and financially between the 25th and the 30th. Are you trying to satisfy someone else rather than yourself? Just because some course of action appears both appropriate and lucrative for others doesn't automatically mean it will apply equally to you.

Destiny dates

Positive: 15, 16, 17, 18

Negative: 26, 29, 30

Mixed: 1, 2, 3, 4, 5, 6, 7, 8, 9, 10, 11, 12, 13, 14, 19, 20, 21, 22, 23, 24, 27, 28

DECEMBER
2011

Highlights of the month

Try to resolve your differences with others because this is the last month of the year and you don't want to be taking bad feelings into the end of year break. You might be finding it hard to let go of past ill feelings with a friend between the 2nd and the 4th. Deep down you want to have 'that talk' with them, but you may be playing hard to get or using mental gymnastics as a way of evading the situation. Demolish the walls, remove the masks, and get real.

Between the 6th and the 10th there is every likelihood that the poor health of someone close to you can impact on your schedule. You will be adjusting your plans to accommodate their needs. Being compassionate may not be all that easy, because there are times when your help may not necessarily improve their situation. Yes, this can be difficult. But at the end of the day, the help you render is to a large extent a means of improving your own spiritual being. Do what you can without too much thought for the result.

Venus once again brings you a touch of class at this closing phase of the year. This is an enjoyable aspect but, between the 12th and the 18th, you may find you have to entertain yourself without the benefit of your closest friend, spouse or partner. Your schedules may not necessarily coincide but this is no reason for you not to enjoy yourself. A little time out on your own could be just what the doctor ordered.

You'll be annoyed between the 19th and 26th, when people in your immediate circle appear rather lazy in doing what needs to be done around the home or workplace. You most certainly have the energy to assert yourself and pick up after others but will not have the mental inclination to do so. Rather than shouting, ranting or raving about your displeasure, quietly asserting yourself will have the desired effect. The key word for you in this period is sharing.

One final planetary aspect of the year relates to Venus and its effect on your finances, which is quite positive, I'm happy to say. There may be a last-minute achievement or acquisition of extra funds.

A pay rise that you had thought was postponed could magically appear, giving you a great sense of relief, especially with extra bills and credit charges at Christmas time.

Romance and friendship

You want new friends and are idealistic about involving yourself in community events, world affairs and maybe even politics. The period of the 1st until the 7th of December brings you in touch with a whole new gamut of social opportunities.

You smell a rat between the 7th and the 10th, but can't quite put your finger on it. You don't trust people and have good reason to believe someone is playing you against someone else. Don't make wild accusations but trust your intuition because the truth will come out eventually.

You're better able to appreciate your own company between the 11th and 14th. Others will think you're playing hard to get, but this is simply not true. You're able to tap into some of your better qualities and feel peace and joy within your own being.

You make a great first impression when Venus transits through your Sun sign from the 16th until the 20th. All of the pleasures of life take on a new meaning. You want to portray yourself in the best possible light and attract a new love or friendship. This person may even be a soulmate with whom you identify immediately on the first meeting.

Your physical health is tiptop leading up to Christmas and, between the 21st and the 27th, you have all the dynamic energy you need to entertain, shop and perform all your duties. This will be a powerful period in which you will be able to fulfil your responsibilities in every department of life.

While on your Christmas break, look into your past. You will connect some of the dots and come up with a revelation in the last few days of the year. The period of the 28th to the 31st is an enlightening one for you and heralds the start of a new year with a great sense of self.

Work and money

Take the offensive on any legal, political or red-tape matter between the 1st and the 9th of December. It will work to your advantage. Your opinions will be solid and even professionals will take note of what you have to say in this regard.

Strike a deal if you have to, but you mustn't let indecision get the better of you between the 10th and the 15th. It's better to be decisive than let your tasks fall behind schedule.

Another party will not wait around long enough to see whether or not you're serious if you don't make them feel you are confident. Don't be unwilling to negotiate between the 16th and the 22nd. You must under no circumstances procrastinate.

Explore what resources are at your disposal to make a radical work change between the 23rd and the 28th. You have far more tools available at your fingertips than you currently believe. Think outside the square.

They say you should 'never argue with an idiot'. Between the 29th and the 31st, someone could drag you down to their level then exhaust you with their inexperience.

Destiny dates

Positive: 1, 11, 12, 13, 14, 15, 16, 17, 18, 27, 28

Negative: 8

Mixed: 2, 3, 4, 6, 7, 9, 10, 19, 20, 21, 22, 23, 24, 25, 26, 29, 30, 31

2011:
Astronumerology

How we spend our days is, of course, how we spend our lives.

—Annie Dillard

The power behind your name

It's hard to believe that your name resonates with a numerical vibration, but it's true! By simply adding the numbers of your name, you can see which planet rules you and what effects your name will have on your life and destiny. According to the ancient Chaldean system of numerology, each number is assigned a planetary energy. Take a look at the chart below to see how each alphabetical letter is connected to a planetary energy:

AIQJY	=	1	Sun
BKR	=	2	Moon
CGLS	=	3	Jupiter
DMT	=	4	Uranus
EHNX	=	5	Mercury
UVW	=	6	Venus
OZ	=	7	Neptune
FP	=	8	Saturn
—	=	9	Mars

The number 9 is not allotted a letter because it is considered 'unknowable'. Once the numbers have been added, establish which single planet rules your name and personal affairs. At this point the number 9 can be used for interpretation. Do you think it's unusual that many famous actors, writers and musicians have modified their names? This is to attract luck and good fortune, which can be made easier by using the energies of a friendlier planet. Try experimenting with the table and see how new names affect you. It's so much fun, and you may even attract greater love, wealth and worldly success!

Look at the following example to work out the power of your name. A person named Andrew Brown would calculate his ruling planet by correlating each letter to a number in the table, like this:

A N D R E W B R O W N
1 5 4 2 5 6 2 2 7 6 5

Now add the numbers like this:

1 + 5 + 4 + 2 + 5 + 6 + 2 + 2 + 7 + 6 + 5 = 45

Then add 4 + 5 = 9

The ruling number of Andrew Brown's name is 9, which is ruled by Mars (see how the 9 can now be used?). Now study the name–number table to reveal the power of your name. The numbers 4 and 5 will also play a secondary role in Andrew's character and destiny, so in this case you would also study the effects of Uranus (4) and Mercury (5).

Name–number table

Your name-number	Ruling planet	Your name characteristics
1	Sun	Attractive personality. Magnetic charm. Superman-, superwoman-like vitality and physical energy. Incredibly active and gregarious. Enjoys outdoor activities and sports. Has friends and individuals in powerful positions. Good government connections. Intelligent, spectacular, flashy and successful. A loyal number for love and relationships.
2	Moon	Feminine and soft, emotional temperament. Fluctuating moods but intuitive, and possibly even clairvoyant abilities. Ingenious nature and kind-hearted expression of feelings. Loves family, mothering and home life. Night owl who probably needs more sleep. Success with the public and/or women generally.
3	Jupiter	Sociable, optimistic number with fortunate destiny. Attracts opportunities without too much effort. Great sense of timing. Religious or spiritual inclinations. Naturally drawn to investigate the meaning of life. Philosophical insight. Enjoys travel and to explore the world and different cultures.
4	Uranus	Volatile character with many peculiar aspects. Likes to experiment and test novel experiences. Forward thinking, with many extraordinary friends. Gets bored easily so needs plenty of inspiring activities. Pioneering, technological and creative. Wilful and obstinate at times. Unforeseen events in life may be positive or negative.

Your name-number	Ruling planet	Your name characteristics
5	Mercury	Sharp wit, quick thinking and with great powers of speech. Extremely active life. Always on the go, living on nervous energy. Youthful outlook and never grows old. Looks younger than actual age. Young friends and humorous disposition. Loves reading and writing. Great communicator.
6	Venus	Delightful and charming. Graceful and eye-catching personality who cherishes and nourishes friends. Very active social life. Musical or creative interests. Great moneymaking opportunities as well as numerous love affairs indicated. Career in the public eye is quite likely. Loves family but is often troubled over divided loyalties with friends.
7	Neptune	Intuitive, spiritual and self-sacrificing nature. Easily duped by those who need help. Loves to dream of life's possibilities. Has healing powers. Dreams are revealing and prophetic. Loves water and will have many journeys in life. Spiritual aspirations dominate worldly desires.
8	Saturn	Hard-working, ambitious person with slow yet certain achievements. Remarkable concentration and self-sacrifice for a chosen objective. Financially focused but generous when a person's trust is gained. Proficient in one's chosen field but is a hard taskmaster. Demands perfection and needs to relax and enjoy life.

Your name-number	Ruling planet	Your name characteristics
9	Mars	Extraordinary physical drive, desires and ambition. Sports and outdoor activities are major keys to health. Confrontational but likes to work and play really hard. Protects and defends family, friends and territory. Individual tastes in life but also self-absorbed. Needs to listen to others' advice to gain greater successes.

Your 2011 planetary ruler

Astrology and numerology are intimately connected. As already shown, each planet rules over a number between 1 and 9. Both your name *and* your birth date are governed by planetary energies.

Simply add the numbers of your birth date and the year in question to find out which planet will control the coming year for you. Here is an example:

If you were born on the 12th of November, add the numerals 1 and 2, for your day of birth, and 1 and 1, for your month of birth, to the year in question, in this case 2011, the current year, like this:

Add 1 + 2 + 1 + 1 + 2 + 0 + 1+ 1 = 9

The planet ruling your individual karma for 2011 will be Mars because this planet rules the number 9.

You can even take your ruling name-number, as shown previously, and add it to the year in question, to throw more light on your coming personal affairs, like this:

A N D R E W B R O W N = 9
Year coming = 2011
Add 9 + 2 + 0 + 1 + 1 = 13
Add 1 + 3 = 4

This is the ruling year number, using your name-number as a basis.

Therefore, study Uranus's (number 4) influence for 2011. Enjoy!

1 is the year of the Sun

Overview

The year 2011 is the commencement of a new cycle for you. Because the Sun rules the number 1, the dominant energy for you in the coming year is solar, which is also connected to the sign of Leo. Expect the coming year to be full of great accomplishments and a high reputation regarding new plans and projects. This is the turning of a new page in the book of your life.

You will experience an uplifting of your physical energies, which makes you ready to assume fresh responsibilities in a new nine-year cycle. Whatever you begin now will surely be successful.

Your physical vitality is strong and your health should improve. If you've been suffering physical ailments, this is the time to improve your physical wellbeing because recovery will be certain.

You're a magnetic person this year, so attracting people into your life won't be difficult. Expect a new circle of friends and possibly even new lovers coming into your life. Get ready to be invited to many parties and different engagements. However, don't go burning the midnight oil because this will overstretch your physical powers.

Don't be too cocky with friends or employers. Maintain some humility, which will make you even more popular throughout 2011.

Love and pleasure

Because this is the commencement of a new cycle, you'll be lucky in love. The Sun also has influence over children, so your family life will also entail more responsibility. Music, art and any other creative activities will be high on your agenda and may be the source of a new romance for you.

Work

Because you are so popular and powerful this year, you won't need to exert too much effort to attract luck, money and new windows of opportunity through your work and group activities. Changes that you make professionally now will pay off, particularly in the coming couple of years. Promotions are likely and don't be surprised to see some extra money coming your way as a pay rise.

Improving your luck

Because Leo and the number 1 are your rulers this year, you'll be especially lucky without too much effort. The months of July and August, being ruled by Leo, are very lucky for you. The 1st, 8th, 15th and 22nd hours of Sundays will be especially lucky. You may also find yourself meeting Leos and they may be able to contribute something to your good fortune throughout the coming year.

This year your lucky numbers are 1, 10, 19 and 28.

2 is the year of the Moon

Overview

The Moon represents emotional, nurturing, mothering and feminine aspects of our natures and 2011 will embody all of these traits in you, and more.

Groundbreaking opportunities in your relationships with family members can be expected. This will offer you immense satisfaction.

Your emotional and mental moods and habits should be examined. If you are reactive in your life, this year will be the perfect time to take greater control of yourself. The sign of Cancer, which is ruled by the Moon, is also very much linked to the number 2 and therefore people born under this sign may have an important role to play in your life.

Love and pleasure

Your home, family life and interpersonal relationships will be the main arenas of activity for you in 2011. You'll be able to take your relationships to a new level. If you haven't had the time to dedicate and devote yourself to the people you love, you can do so throughout the coming twelve months.

Thinking of moving? These lunar energies may cause you to change your residence or renovate your current home to make your living circumstances much more in tune with your mind and your heart.

Work

Working from home can be a great idea—or at least, spending more time alone to focus your attention on what you really want—will benefit you professionally. You need to control yourself and think carefully about how you are going to achieve your desired goals.

Women can be a source of opportunity for you and, if you're looking for a change in work, use your connections, especially feminine ones, to achieve success.

Improving your luck

The sign of Cancer being ruled by the Moon also has a connection with Mondays and therefore this will be one of your luckier days throughout 2011. The month of July is also one in which some of your dreams may come true. The 1st, 8th, 15th and 22nd hours on Mondays are successful times. Pay special attention to the new and full Moons in 2011.

The numbers 2, 11, 20, 29 and 38 are lucky for you.

3 is the year of Jupiter

Overview

Number 3 is one of the luckiest numbers, being ruled by Jupiter. Therefore, 2011 should be an exciting and expansive year for you. The planet Jupiter and the sign of Sagittarius will dominate the affairs of your life.

Under the number 3 you'll desire a richer, deeper and broader experience of life and as a result your horizons will also be much broader. You have the ability to gain money, to increase your popularity, and to have loads of fun.

Generosity is one of the key words of the number 3 and you're likely to help others fulfil their desires, too. There is an element of humanity and self-sacrifice indicated by this number and so the more spiritual and compassionate elements of your personality will bubble to the surface. You can improve yourself as a person generally, and this is also a year when your good karma should be used unselfishly to help others as well as yourself.

Love and pleasure

Exploring the world through travel will be an important component of your social and romantic life throughout 2011. It's quite likely that, through your travels and your contacts in other places, you may meet people who will spur you on to love and romance.

You'll be a bit of a gambler in 2011 and the number 3 will make you speculative. This could mean a few false starts in the area of love, but don't be afraid to explore the signs of human possibilities. You may just meet your soulmate as a result.

If you're currently in a relationship, you can deepen your love for each other and push the relationship to new heights.

Work

This is a fortunate year for you. The year 2011 brings you opportunities and success. Your employers will listen to your ideas and accommodate your requests for extra money.

Starting a new job is likely, possibly even your own business. You will try something big and bold. Have no fear: success is on your side.

Improving your luck

As long as you don't push yourself too hard you will have a successful year. Maintain a first-class plan and stick to it. Be realistic about what you are capable of. On the 1st, 8th, 15th and 24th hours of Thursdays, your intuition will make you lucky.

Your lucky numbers this year are 3, 12, 21 and 30. March and December are lucky months. The year 2011 will bring you some unexpected surprises.

4 is the year of Uranus

Overview

Expect the unexpected in 2011. This is a year when you achieve extraordinary things but have to make serious choices between several opportunities. You need to break free of your own past self-limitations, off-load any baggage that is hindering you, in both your personal and professional lives. It's an independent year and self-development will be important to achieving success.

Discipline is one of your key words for 2011. Maintain an orderly lifestyle, a clear-cut routine, and get more sleep. You'll gain strong momentum to fulfil yourself in each and every department of your life.

Love and pleasure

You may be dissatisfied with the current status quo in your relationships, so you're likely to break free and experiment with something different. Your relationships will be anything but dull or routine. You're looking for someone who is prepared to explore emotional and sexual landscapes.

Your social life will also be exciting and you'll meet unusual people who will open your eyes to new and fruitful activities. Spiritual and self-help activities will also capture your attention and enable you to make the most of your new friendships.

Work

The number 4 is modern, progressive and ruled by Uranus. Due to this, all sorts of technological gadgets, computing and Internet activities will play a significant role in your professional life. Move ahead with the times and upgrade your professional skills, because any new job you attempt will require it.

Work could be a little overwhelming, especially if you've not been accustomed to keeping a tight schedule. Be more efficient with your time.

Groups are important to your work efforts this year, so utilise your friends in finding a position you desire. Listen to their advice and become more of a team player because this will be a short cut in your pathway to success.

Improving your luck

Slow your pace this year because being impulsive will only cause you to make errors and waste time. 'Patience is a virtue', but in your case, when being ruled by the number 4, patience will be even more important for you.

The 1st, 8th, 15th and 20th hours of any Saturday will be very lucky for you in 2011.

Your lucky numbers are 4, 13, 22 and 31.

5 is the year of Mercury

Overview

Owing to the rulership of 2011 by the number 5, your intellectual and communicative abilities will be at a peak. Your imagination is also greatly stimulated by Mercury and so exciting new ideas will be constantly churning in your mind.

The downside of the number 5 is its convertible nature, which means it's likely that, when crunch times come and you have to make decisions, it will be difficult to do so. Get all your information together before drawing a firm conclusion. Develop a strong will and unshakable attitude to overcome distractions.

Contracts, new job offers and other agreements also need to be studied carefully before coming to any decision. Business skills and communication are the key words for your life in 2011.

Love and pleasure

One of the contributing factors to your love life in 2011 is service. You must learn to give to your partner if you wish to receive. There may be a change in your routine and this will be necessary if you are to keep your love life exciting, fresh and alive.

You could be critical, so be careful if you are trying to correct the behaviour of others. You'll be blunt and this will alienate you from your peers. Maintain some control over your critical mind before handing out your opinions.

You are likely to become interested in beautifying yourself and looking your best.

Work

Your ideas will be at the forefront of your professional activities this year. You are fast, capable and also innovative in the way you conduct yourself in the workplace. If you need to make any serious changes, however, it is best to think twice before 'jumping out of the pan and into the fire'.

Travel will also be a big component of your working life this year, and you can expect a hectic schedule with lots of flitting about here, there and everywhere. Pace yourself.

Improving your luck

Your greatest fortune will be in communicating ideas. Don't jump from one idea to another too quickly, though, because this will dilute your success.

Listen to your body signals as well because your health is strongly governed by the number 5. Sleep well, eat sensibly and exercise regularly to rebuild your resilience and strength.

The 1st, 8th, 15th and 20th hours of Wednesdays are your luckiest, so schedule your meetings and other important social engagements at these times.

Throughout 2011 your lucky numbers are 5, 14, 23 and 32.

6 is the year of Venus

Overview

The number 6 can be summed up in one beautiful four-letter word: LOVE! Venus rules 6 and is well known for its sensual, romantic and marital overtones. The year 2011 offers you all of this and more. If you're looking for a soulmate, it's likely to happen under a 6 vibration.

This year is a period of hard work to improve your security and finances. Saving money, cutting costs and looking to your future will be important. Keep in mind that this is a year of sharing love *and* material resources.

Love and pleasure

Romance is a key feature of 2011 and, if you're currently in a relationship, you can expect it to become more fulfilling. Important karmic connections are likely during this 6 year for those of you who are not yet married or in a relationship.

Beautify yourself, get a new hairstyle, work on looking your best through improving your fashion sense, new styles of jewellery and getting out there and showing the world what you're made of. This is a year in which your social engagements result in better relationships.

Try not to overdo it, because Venus has a tendency towards excess. Moderation in all things is important in a Venus year 6.

Work

The year 2011 will stimulate your knowledge about finance and your future security. You'll be capable of cutting back expenses and learning how to stretch a dollar. There could be surplus cash this year, increased income or some additional bonuses. You'll use this money to improve your living circumstances because home life is also important under a 6 year.

Your domestic situation could also be tied in with your work. During this year of Venus, your business and social activities will overlap.

Improving your luck

Money will flow as long as you keep an open mind

and positive attitude. Remove negative personality traits obstructing you from greater luck. Be moderate in your actions and don't focus primarily on money. Your spiritual needs also require attention.

The 1st, 8th, 15th and 20th hours on Fridays are extremely lucky for you this year and new opportunities can arise when you least expect it.

The numbers 6, 15, 24 and 33 will generally increase your luck.

7 is the year of Neptune

Overview

Under a 7 year of Neptune, your spiritual and intuitive powers peak. Although your ideals seem clearer and more spiritually orientated, others may not understand your purpose. Develop the power of your convictions to balance your inner ideals with the practical demands of life.

You must learn to let go of your past emotional issues, break through these barriers to improve your life and your relationships this year. This might require you to sever ties with some of the usual people you have become accustomed to being with, which will give you the chance to focus on your own inner needs.

Love and pleasure

Relationships may be demanding and it's at this point in your life that you'll realise you have to give something to yourself as well, not just give to others indefinitely. If the people that matter most in your life are not reciprocating and meeting your needs, you'll have to make some important changes this year.

When it comes to helping others, pick your mark. Not everyone is deserving of the love and resources you have to offer. If you're indiscriminate, you could find yourself with egg on your face if you have been taken advantage of. Be firm, but compassionate.

Work

Compassionate work best describes 2011 under a 7 year. But the challenges of your professional life give you greater insight into yourself and the ability to see clearly what you *don't* want in your life any more. Remove what is unnecessary and this will pave the way for brighter successes.

Caring for and helping others will be important because your work will now bring you to a point where you realise that selfishness, money and security are not the only important things in life. Helping others will be part of your process, which will bring excellent benefits.

Improving your luck

Self-sacrifice, along with discipline and personal discrimination, bring luck. Don't let people use you because this will only result in more emotional baggage. The law of karma states that what you give, you will receive in greater measure; but sometimes the more you give, the more people take, too. Remember that.

The 1st, 8th, 15th and 20th hours of Tuesdays will be lucky times this year.

Try the numbers 7, 16, 25 and 34 to increase your luck.

8 is the year of Saturn

Overview

The number 8 is the most practical of the numbers, being ruled by Saturn and Capricorn. This means that your discipline, attention to detail and hard work will help you achieve your goals. Remaining solitary and not being overly involved with people will help you focus on things that matter. Resisting temptation will be part of your challenge this year, but doing so will also help you become a better person.

Love and pleasure

Balance your personal affairs with work. If you pay too much attention to your work, finances and your professional esteem, you may be missing out on the simple things in life, mainly love and affection.

Being responsible is certainly a great way to show your love to the ones who matter to you, such as your family members. But if you're concerned only with work and no play, it makes for a very dull family life. Make a little more time to enjoy your family and friends and schedule some time off on the weekends so you can enjoy the journey, not just the goal.

Work

You can make a lot of money this year and, if you've been focused on your work for the last couple of years, this is a time when money should flow to you. The Chinese believe the number 8 is indeed the money number and can bring you the fruits of your hard labour.

Because you're cautious and resourceful you'll be able to save more this year, but try not to be too stingy with your money.

Under an 8 year you'll take on new responsibilities. You mustn't do this for the sake of looking good. If you truly like the work that is being offered, by all means take it. But if it's simply for the sake of ego, you'll be very disappointed.

Improving your luck

This year you could be a little reluctant to try new things. But if you are overly cautious, you may miss opportunities. Don't act impulsively on what is being offered, of course, but do be open to trying some alternative things as well.

Be gentle and kind to yourself. By pampering yourself you send out a strong signal to the universe that you are deserving of some rewards.

The 1st, 8th, 15th and 20th hours of Saturdays are the best times for you in 2011.

The numbers 1, 8, 17, 26 and 35 are your lucky numbers.

9 is the year of Mars

Overview

The year 2011 is the final year of a nine-year cycle and this will be dominated by Aries and Mars. You'll be rushing madly to complete many things, so be careful not to overstep the mark of your capability. Work hard but balance your life with adequate rest.

In your relationships you will realise that you are at odds with your partner and want different things. This is the time to talk it out. If the communication between you isn't flowing well, you might find yourself leaving the relationship and moving on to bigger or better things. Worthwhile communication is a two-way street that will benefit both of you.

Love and pleasure

Mars is very pushy and infuses the number 9 with this kind of energy. The upshot is you need to be gentle in conveying your ideas and offering your views. Avoid arguments if you want to improve your relationships.

If you feel it's time for a change, discuss it with your partner. You can work through this feeling together and create an exciting new pathway for your love life. Don't get too angry with the little things in life. Get out and play some sport if you feel you are inappropriately taking out your bad moods on the ones you love.

Work

You have an intense drive and strong capability to achieve anything you choose in 2011. But be careful you don't overdo things, because you are prone to pushing yourself too far. Pace your deadlines, stagger the workload and, if possible, delegate some of the more menial tasks to others so you'll have time to do your own work properly.

Number 9 has an element of leadership associated with it, so you may be asked to take over and lead the group. This brings with it added responsibility but can also inspire you greatly.

Improving your luck

Restlessness is one of the problems that the number 9 brings with it, so you must learn to meditate and pacify your mind so you can take advantage of what the universe has to offer. If you're scattered in your energies, your attention will miss vital opportunities and your relationships could also become rather problematic as well.

Your health and vitality will remain strong as long as you rest adequately and find suitable outlets for your tension.

The 1st, 8th, 15th and 20th hours of Tuesdays will be lucky for you throughout 2011. Your lucky numbers are 9, 18, 27 and 36.

CAPRICORN

2011:
Your Daily Planner

*My life has no purpose, no direction, no aim, no
meaning, and yet I'm happy. I can't figure it out.
What am I doing right?*

—Charles Schulz

There is a little-known branch of astrology called
electional astrology, and it can help you select the
most appropriate times for many of your day-to-day
activities.

Ancient astrologers understood the planetary
patterns and how they impacted on each of us. This
allowed them to suggest the best possible times
to start various important activities. Many farmers
today still use this approach: they understand the
phases of the Moon, and attest to the fact that
planting seeds on certain lunar days produces a far
better crop than planting on other days.

The following section covers many areas of day-
to-day life, and uses the cycles of the Moon and the
combined strength of the other planets to work out
the best times to start different types of activity.

So to create your own personal almanac, first
select the activity you are interested in, then quickly
scan the year for the best months to start it. When
you have selected the month, you can finetune
your timing by finding the best specific dates. You
can then be sure that the planetary energies will
be in sync with you, offering you the best possible
outcome.

Coupled with what you know about your monthly
and weekly trends, the daily planner can be a

powerful tool to help you capitalise on opportunities that come your way this year.

Good luck, and may the planets bless you with great success, fortune and happiness in 2011!

Starting activities

How many times have you made a new year's resolution to begin a diet or be a better person in your relationships? And how many times has it not worked out? Well, part of the reason may be that you started out at the wrong time, because how successful you are is strongly influenced by the position of the Moon and the planets when you begin a particular activity. You will be more successful with the following endeavours if you start them on the days indicated.

Relationships

We all feel more empowered on some days than on others. This is because the planets have some power over us—their movement and their relationships to each other determine the ebb and flow of our energies. And our level of self-confidence and our sense of romantic magnetism play an important part in the way we behave in relationships.

Your daily planner tells you the ideal dates for meeting new friends, initiating a love affair, spending time with family and loved ones—it even tells you the most appropriate times for sexual encounters.

You'll be surprised at how much more impact you can make in your relationships when you tune yourself in to the planetary energies on these special dates.

Falling in love or restoring love

During these times you could expect favourable energies to be present to meet your soulmate. Or, if you've had difficulty in a relationship, you can approach the one you love to rekindle both your and their emotional responses.

January	8, 9, 10, 13, 14, 15, 18, 19, 20, 21
February	4, 5, 6, 9, 10, 11, 14
March	1, 9, 10, 14, 15, 16, 17
April	5, 6, 17, 25, 26
May	3, 4, 6, 7, 8, 9, 10, 11, 14, 15, 22, 23, 24
June	1, 11, 18, 19, 20, 28, 29, 30
July	7, 8, 26, 27, 30, 31
August	3, 12, 13, 14, 22, 23, 27, 31
September	1, 18, 19, 20, 26, 27, 28, 29, 30
October	12, 13, 17, 18, 25, 26, 29, 30, 31
November	2, 3, 4, 5, 6, 9, 17, 29
December	3, 7, 8, 11, 14, 15, 18, 19, 29, 30

Special times with friends and family

Socialising, partying and having a good time with those you enjoy being with is highly favourable under the following dates. These are also excellent days to spend time with family and loved ones in a domestic environment:

January	17, 20, 21
February	2, 9, 10, 11, 18, 19, 20, 21, 22, 23, 24, 28
March	1, 11, 14, 16, 17, 20
April	2, 11, 12, 21, 22, 26
May	6, 9, 10, 11, 14, 15, 22, 23, 24
June	4, 8, 10, 12, 19, 20, 25, 26, 28
July	7, 8, 16, 23, 30, 31
August	4, 5, 6, 7, 13, 20, 27, 31
September	1, 6, 18, 19, 20, 29, 30
October	1, 16, 17, 25, 26
November	2, 12, 13, 17, 26, 29
December	11, 14, 15, 18, 19, 27, 28

Healing or resuming a relationship

If you're trying to get back together with the one you love and need a heart-to-heart or deep and meaningful conversation, you can try the following dates to do so:

January	2, 3, 4, 5, 6, 7, 8, 9, 10, 11, 12, 13, 14, 15, 16, 17, 18, 19, 20, 21, 28
February	1, 2, 4, 5, 6, 7, 21, 22, 23, 24, 28
March	1, 8, 9, 10, 11, 14, 16, 17, 18, 19, 20
April	2, 11, 12, 26
May	1, 6, 7, 8, 9, 10, 11, 12, 13, 15, 19, 22, 24, 25, 26, 27, 28
June	5, 12, 14, 15, 16, 19, 23, 25, 26, 27, 28, 29, 30
July	4, 6, 7, 8, 9, 10, 16, 19, 21, 23, 28, 29, 30, 31
August	1, 2, 3, 13, 15, 16, 20, 27, 29, 30, 31
September	1, 2, 3, 4, 5, 6, 13, 15, 16, 17, 18, 19, 20, 21, 22, 23, 25, 28, 29
October	12, 13, 15, 16, 17, 18, 25, 27, 29
November	2, 4, 5, 6, 15, 16, 17, 26, 29
December	11, 19, 20, 21, 22, 23

Sexual encounters

Physical and sexual energies are well favoured on the following dates. The energies of the planets enhance your moments of intimacy during these times:

January	2, 3, 4, 5, 6, 7, 8, 9, 10, 11, 12, 20, 21, 25
February	7, 8, 18, 19, 20, 21
March	1, 8, 11, 14, 20, 21

April	4, 11, 12, 25, 26, 27, 28, 29
May	2, 9, 10, 11, 14, 15, 22, 23, 24
June	1, 11, 12, 18, 19, 20, 28, 29, 30
July	7, 8, 16, 19, 20, 21, 23, 30
August	3, 12, 13, 14, 20, 22, 27, 31
September	1, 18, 19, 20, 29, 30
October	1, 13, 15, 18, 19, 20, 21, 22, 25, 26
November	2, 3, 11, 15, 16, 17, 18, 21, 22
December	5, 6, 12, 13, 14, 15, 18, 19

Health and wellbeing

Your aura and life force are susceptible to the movements of the planets; in particular, they respond to the phases of the Moon.

The following dates are the most appropriate times to begin a diet, have cosmetic surgery, or seek medical advice. They also tell you when the best times are to help others.

Feeling of wellbeing

Your physical as well as your mental alertness should be strong on these following dates. You can plan your activities and expect a good response from others:

January	7, 9, 10, 11, 12, 13, 14, 18, 20, 21
February	4, 18, 19, 20, 21, 22, 23, 24

March	16, 17, 19, 20
April	2, 7, 12, 20, 22, 25, 26
May	9, 10, 11, 14, 15, 16, 17, 22, 24, 25
June	4, 8, 10, 11, 12, 16, 17, 18, 19, 20, 21, 23, 25, 26
July	7, 8, 9, 10, 26, 27, 30
August	3, 4, 5, 6, 12, 13, 14, 17, 19, 22, 27, 31
September	1, 13, 26, 27, 28, 29, 30
October	1, 16, 17, 25, 26, 30, 31
November	1, 2, 3, 4, 5, 6, 17, 29
December	4, 11, 14, 15, 18, 19, 21, 22, 23, 30

Healing and medical

These times are good for approaching others who have expertise when you need some deeper understanding. They are also favourable for any sort of healing or medication, and for making appointments with doctors or psychologists. Planning surgery around these dates should bring good results.

Often giving up our time and energy to assist others doesn't necessarily result in the expected outcome. By lending a helping hand to a friend on the following dates, the results should be favourable:

January	1, 2, 3, 4, 5, 6, 7, 8, 14, 15, 16, 17, 18, 19, 20, 21, 22, 23, 24, 25, 26, 27, 28, 29, 31
February	3, 4, 5, 6, 7, 8, 9, 10, 13, 15, 16, 17, 18, 19, 21, 22, 23, 24, 25, 26, 27
March	4, 9, 10, 11, 12, 15, 16
April	2, 9, 10, 11, 12, 13, 14, 15, 16, 17, 18, 19, 20, 21, 22, 23, 24, 25, 26, 27, 28, 29, 30
May	1, 2, 3, 4, 5, 6, 8, 9, 10, 11, 12, 13, 14, 15, 16, 17, 18, 19, 20, 21, 22, 23, 24, 25, 30
June	23, 26, 28
July	3, 10, 11, 12
August	7, 8, 9, 10, 11, 12, 13, 14, 15, 16, 20, 21, 25
September	23, 25, 26, 27
October	20, 21, 22, 23, 24, 25, 26, 27, 28, 29, 30, 31
November	1, 2, 3, 4, 5, 6, 7, 8, 9, 10, 11, 12, 13, 14, 15, 16, 17, 18, 19, 20, 21, 22, 23, 24, 25, 30
December	1, 2, 3, 4, 5, 6, 7, 8, 9, 10, 30

Money

Money is an important part of life, and involves lots of decisions—decisions about borrowing, investing, spending. The ideal times for transactions are very much influenced by the planets, and whether your investment or nest egg grows or doesn't grow can often be linked to timing. Making your decisions on the following dates could give you a whole new perspective on your financial future:

Managing wealth and money

To build your nest egg it's a good time to open a bank account and invest money on the following dates:

January	2, 3, 9, 10, 11, 12, 13, 14, 15, 16, 17, 18, 19, 20, 21, 22, 24, 28
February	3, 4, 5, 6, 7, 8, 9, 11, 13, 14, 16, 18, 19, 20, 21, 22, 23, 24, 25, 26, 27
March	4, 8, 11, 12, 13, 14, 16, 17, 18, 19
April	2, 7, 8, 9, 10, 11, 12, 13, 16, 17, 18, 19, 20, 21, 22, 23, 24, 25
May	1, 6, 7, 8, 9, 10, 11, 12, 13, 14, 15, 16, 17, 18, 19, 20, 21, 22, 23, 24, 25, 30
June	3, 4, 5, 8, 16, 17, 18, 19, 20, 23, 25, 26, 27, 28
July	4, 5, 6, 7, 8, 9, 10, 11, 12, 16, 23, 25, 28, 29, 30, 31
August	1, 2, 3, 4, 5, 6, 7, 8, 9, 10, 11, 12, 13, 14, 15, 16, 17, 19, 20, 30, 31
September	2, 11, 13, 15, 23, 25, 26, 27, 28, 29, 30
October	1, 2, 3, 4, 5, 6, 7, 8, 13, 14, 15, 16, 17, 18, 19, 21, 24, 25, 26, 27, 28, 29, 30, 31

| November | 2, 3, 4, 5, 6, 7, 9, 11, 12, 13, 14, 15, 16, 17, 18, 19, 20, 23, 25, 29 |
| December | 6, 13, 19, 26, 31 |

Spending

It's always fun to spend, but the following dates are more in tune with this activity and are likely to give you better results:

January	8, 9, 10, 11, 12, 13, 14, 15
February	9, 11, 18, 19
March	9
April	22
May	6, 7, 8, 9, 10, 11, 12, 13, 14, 17, 18, 19, 20, 21, 22, 23, 24
June	4, 8, 10, 11, 12, 14, 16, 17, 19
July	6, 7, 8, 9, 10, 11, 31
August	1, 2, 3, 4, 5, 6, 15, 16, 17, 18, 19, 30, 31
September	1, 2, 3, 4, 17, 19, 28, 29, 30
October	12, 13, 14, 15, 16, 17, 18, 19, 27, 28, 29, 30, 31
November	2, 3, 4, 5, 6, 7
December	3, 4, 5, 22, 23

Selling

If you're thinking of selling something, whether it is

small or large, consider the following dates as ideal times to do so:

January	2, 3, 9, 10, 11, 12, 13, 14, 15, 16, 17, 18, 19, 20, 22, 24, 28
February	3, 4, 5, 6, 7, 8, 9, 11, 13, 14, 16, 18, 19, 20, 21, 22, 23, 24, 25, 26, 27
March	4, 8, 11, 12, 13, 14, 16, 17, 18, 19
April	2, 7, 8, 9, 10, 11, 12, 13, 16, 17, 18, 19, 20, 21, 22, 23, 24
May	1, 6, 7, 8, 9, 10, 11, 12, 13, 14, 15, 16, 17, 18, 19, 20, 21, 22, 23, 24, 25, 26, 30
June	3, 4, 5, 8, 16, 17, 18, 19, 20, 23, 25, 26, 27, 28
July	4, 5, 6, 7, 8, 9, 10, 11, 12, 16, 23, 25, 28, 29, 30, 31
August	1, 2, 3, 4, 5, 6, 7, 8, 9, 10, 11, 12, 13, 14, 15, 16, 17, 19, 20, 30, 31
September	2, 11, 13, 15, 23, 25, 26, 27, 28, 29, 30
October	1, 2, 3, 4, 5, 6, 7, 8, 13, 14, 15, 16, 17, 18, 19, 21, 24, 25, 26, 27, 28, 29, 30, 31
November	2, 3, 4, 5, 6, 7, 9, 11, 12, 13, 14, 15, 16, 17, 18, 19, 20, 23, 25, 29
December	2, 3, 4, 5, 6, 7, 11, 30

Borrowing

Few of us like to borrow money, but if you must, taking out a loan on the following dates will be positive:

January	1, 20, 21, 26, 27, 28, 31
February	1, 2, 22, 23, 24
March	1, 22, 23, 26, 27, 29, 31
April	1, 18, 19, 22, 23, 24, 25, 26, 27, 28, 29
May	17, 18, 19, 20, 21, 22, 23, 24, 25, 26
June	16, 17, 18, 19, 22
July	15, 16, 28, 29, 30
August	15, 16, 24, 25, 26, 27, 28
September	21, 22
October	21
November	14, 15, 16, 17, 23, 24
December	12, 13, 14, 15, 20, 21, 22, 23, 24

Speculation and investment

To invest your money and get a good return on that investment try taking a punt on the following dates:

January	3, 4, 5, 11, 12, 18, 19, 24, 25, 31
February	1, 7, 8, 14, 15, 20, 21, 27, 28
March	6, 7, 8, 14, 15, 20, 21, 26, 27

April	2, 3, 4, 10, 11, 16, 17, 22, 23, 24, 30
May	1, 7, 8, 14, 15, 20, 21, 27, 28, 29
June	3, 4, 5, 10, 11, 16, 17, 23, 24, 25
July	1, 2, 7, 8, 14, 15, 21, 22, 28, 29
August	3, 4, 10, 11, 17, 18, 19, 24, 25, 26, 31
September	1, 6, 7, 13, 14, 15, 21, 22, 27, 28
October	3, 4, 5, 11, 12, 18, 19, 25, 26, 31
November	1, 7, 8, 14, 15, 16, 21, 22, 27, 28
December	4, 5, 6, 12, 13, 18, 19, 25, 26, 31

Work and education

Your career is important to you, and continual improvement of your skills is therefore also crucial, professionally, mentally and socially. These dates will help you find out the most appropriate times to improve your professional talents and commence new work or education associated with your work.

You may need to decide when to start learning a new skill, when to ask for a promotion, and even when to make an important career change. Here are the days when your mental and educational power is strong.

Learning new skills

Educational pursuits are lucky and bring good results on the following dates:

January	16, 17
February	12, 13
March	11, 12, 13, 18, 19
April	7, 8, 9, 14, 15
May	5, 6, 12, 13
June	2, 8, 9, 14, 15
July	5, 6, 11, 12, 13
August	1, 2, 8, 9, 29, 30
September	4, 5
October	1, 2, 29, 30
November	25, 26
December	9, 10

Changing career path or profession

If you're feeling stuck and need to move into a new professional activity, changing jobs is recommended at these times:

January	4, 5, 13, 14, 15
February	9, 10, 11
March	1, 2, 3, 9, 10, 11, 12, 18, 19, 20, 21
April	5, 6, 7, 8, 9, 14, 15, 16, 17, 25, 26
May	3, 4, 12, 13, 22, 23, 24
June	1, 2, 8, 9, 18, 19, 20, 28, 29, 30

July	5, 6, 14, 26, 27
August	3, 4, 10, 11, 22, 23, 29, 30, 31
September	1, 6, 7, 8, 9, 10, 18, 19, 20, 27, 28
October	3, 4, 5, 16, 17, 25, 26, 31
November	1, 2, 3, 9, 10, 29, 30
December	1, 7, 8, 9, 10, 11, 18, 19, 25, 26, 27, 28

Promotion, professional focus and hard work

To increase your mental focus and achieve good results from the work you do; promotions are also likely on the dates that follow:

January	3, 9, 10, 11, 12, 13, 14, 18
February	22, 23, 24, 25, 26, 27, 28
March	8, 10, 11, 13, 14, 16, 17, 18, 19
April	11, 12
May	6, 7, 8, 9, 10, 11, 12, 13, 15, 16, 17, 19, 21, 22, 23, 24
June	4, 5, 8, 11, 12, 14, 15, 16, 17, 19
July	16, 18, 19, 20, 23, 24, 25, 28, 29, 30
August	1, 2, 14, 15, 16, 17, 19, 30
September	1, 2, 3, 4, 5, 6, 11, 13, 16, 17, 19
October	13, 15, 16, 17, 18, 19
November	2, 4, 5, 6, 7, 12
December	25, 26

Travel

Setting out on a holiday or adventurous journey is exciting. Here are the most favourable times for doing this. Travel on the following dates is likely to give you a sense of fulfilment:

January	9, 10, 11, 12, 16, 17, 18, 19
February	4, 5, 6, 7, 15
March	19
April	7, 8, 9, 10, 11
May	15
June	4, 8, 10, 11
July	1, 5, 6
August	1, 2, 3, 4, 8
September	27, 28
October	1, 3, 4, 29, 30, 31
November	1, 4, 5, 6
December	3, 4, 5, 25, 29, 30

Beauty and grooming

Believe it or not, cutting your hair or nails has a powerful effect on your body's electromagnetic energy. If you cut your hair or nails at the wrong time of the month, you can reduce your level of vitality significantly. Use these dates to ensure you optimise your energy levels by staying in tune with the stars:

Haircuts

January	1, 2, 8, 9, 10, 16, 17, 28, 29, 30
February	25, 26
March	4, 5, 11, 12, 13, 14, 25, 31
April	1, 7, 8, 9, 20, 21, 27, 28, 29
May	5, 6, 18, 19, 25, 26
June	1, 2, 14, 15, 21, 22, 28, 29, 30
July	11, 12, 13, 18, 19, 20, 26, 27
August	8, 9, 15, 16, 22, 23
September	4, 5, 11, 12, 18, 19, 20
October	1, 2, 8, 9, 10, 16, 17, 29, 30
November	4, 5, 6, 12, 13, 25, 26
December	2, 3, 9, 10, 11, 23, 24, 29, 30

Cutting nails

January	11, 12, 13, 14, 15, 18, 19, 20, 21
February	7, 8, 9, 10, 11, 14, 16
March	6, 8, 9, 10, 14, 15
April	2, 3, 5, 6
May	4, 7, 8, 9, 10, 11, 27, 28, 29, 30, 31
June	3, 4, 5, 6, 7, 23, 25, 26, 27
July	1, 2, 3, 21, 22, 23, 24, 25, 28, 29, 30, 31

August	17, 19, 20, 24, 25, 26
September	13, 16, 17, 21, 22, 23, 24
October	11, 13, 15, 18, 19, 20, 21, 22
November	15, 16, 17, 18
December	4, 5, 6, 7, 8

Therapies, massage and self-pampering

January	1, 2, 8, 9, 10, 16, 17, 28, 29, 30
February	5, 6, 12, 13, 25, 26
March	4, 5, 11, 12, 13, 24, 25, 31
April	1, 7, 8, 9, 20, 21, 27, 28, 29
May	5, 6, 18, 19, 25, 26
June	1, 2, 14, 15, 21, 22, 28, 29, 30
July	11, 12, 13, 18, 19, 20, 26, 27
August	8, 9, 15, 16, 22, 23
September	4, 5, 11, 12, 18, 19, 20
October	1, 2, 8, 9, 10, 16, 17, 29, 30
November	4, 5, 6, 12, 13, 25, 26
December	2, 3, 9, 10, 11, 23, 24, 29, 30

VEB/M&B/RTL3

Discover Pure Reading Pleasure with

**Visit the Mills & Boon website for all
the latest in romance**

🌹 **Buy** all the latest
releases, backlist
and eBooks

🌹 **Find out** more
about our authors
and their books

🌹 **Join** our community
and chat to authors
and other readers

🌹 **Free** online reads
from your favourite
authors

🌹 **Win** with our
fantastic online
competitions

🌹 **Sign** up for our
free monthly
eNewsletter

🌹 **Tell us** what you
think by signing up to
our reader panel

🌹 **Rate** and review
books with our star
system

www.millsandboon.co.uk

 Follow us at twitter.com/millsandboonuk

 Become a fan at facebook.com/romancehq